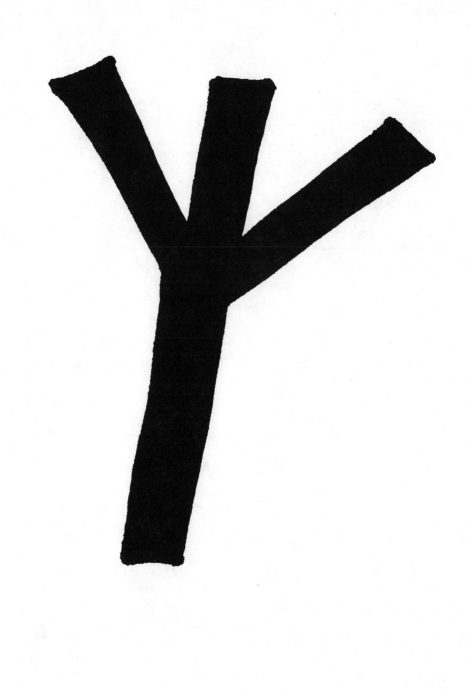

Family Counseling: An Annotated Bibliography

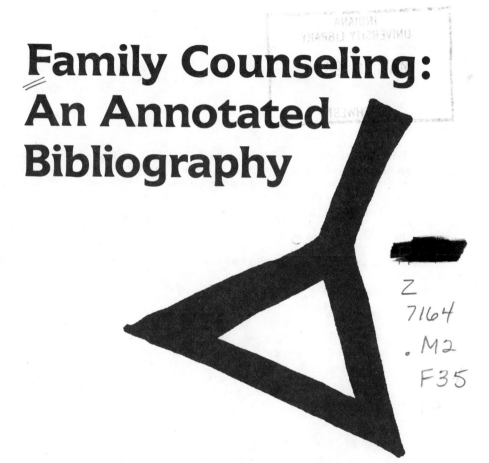

University Research Corporation

Oelgeschlager, Gunn & Hain, Publishers, Inc.
Cambridge, Massachusetts

Edited by Kristi Brown
Literature Searches by Mary Iglehart,
   Suzanne Hardin, and Pat Place
Introduction by John Peters, MSW

International Standard Book Number: 0-89946-094-1

Library of Congress Catalog Card Number: 81-9644

Printed in West Germany

KM
5-17-83

Contents

Acknowledgments

We should like to acknowledge the help of those University Research Corporation staff members who contributed greatly to the development of this book. The following persons--whose expertise in various aspects of family counseling as teachers, trainers, clinicians, consultants, and researchers enabled us to focus our inquiries into the latest state-of-the-art documents and publications for inclusion--contributed through screening articles, creating categories of compilation, and providing background information on the history and development of the family counseling/therapy schools of thought and on those recognized professional disciplines that make up the body of family counseling practitioners: William Barse, Ann Bauman, Denise Crute, James Dahl, Patricia Delaney, Lewis Eigen, Ed.D., Leo Fishel, M.P.H., Hyman Frankel, Ph.D., Roberta Glick, M.S.W., Trudy Hamby, Leroy Jones, Joseph Kelly, Warren Kinsman, Norman LaCharite, Ph.D., William Link, Freddie Martin, Ph.D., John Mongeon, Mary Millar, Lenne Miller, John Peters, M.S.W., Joanne Philleo, M.S.W., Stanley Scheyer, M.D., Myrna Seidman, M.P.H., and Sheldon Steinberg, Ed.D.

The actual literature searches were conducted by research librarians Mary Iglehart, Suzanne Hardin, and Pat Place, and major portions of the writing and editing were done by Kristi Brown and Dana Murphy. Design and formatting assistance was provided by Patricia Bryant.

The many hours of work required to produce a comprehensive compilation of available research and practice literature could only have been accomplished with the ongoing assistance of these content and technical personnel.

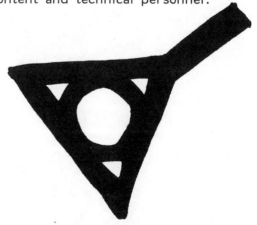

Introduction

The history of family counseling as such is a relatively short one in comparison to other types of counseling. Yet, it is already marked by the same diversity of fundamental assumptions and values, techniques, locus, goals, and pre- and co-requisite prescriptions--in short, by all of the attributes that characterize all other types of intervention into the behaviors and inner workings of human beings.

If there is one characteristic distinguishing family counseling from all other current counseling approaches, it is that the focus of effort--the object of interventive activity--is no longer on the solitary individual human being, whether viewed as shaped by environments or not. This distinctive mark is stated negatively because of differing definitions given or implied by writers, practitioners, and theoreticians of what exactly constitutes a "family."

Some practitioners of the art subsume under the rubric of "family" any unit of two or more individuals related by some clear physical, psychological, and/or social bonds which last over some period of time and are more than casual or superficial, as defined at least by the parties to the relationship. Thus, the focus of family counseling may embrace units of treatment or intervention as disparate as an unmarried mother and her child, a homosexual pair with an adopted child, or an extended family the size of a clan. Implicit in many of the notions of "family" is the idea that the relationships of the members are or should be nurturing and supportive in some respect.

In any event, the key shift which family counseling reflects is a shift away from the traditional and pervasive focus on the individual person that is found in nearly all therapies going back to the very beginnings of the activity called "counseling."

This shift also signals an opening up of the already diverse bases of all types of counseling to knowledge drawn from fields traditionally untapped, such as linguistics, sociology, cybernetics, and systems theory. From the several frameworks of family counseling, a great leap has been taken not only away from one unit of treatment to another, but also across boundaries of knowledge.

The titles in this annotated bibliography reveal this refocus of human intervention away from the private to the social entity. In this respect, it betokens a "making public" of private matters. The titles also show the extraordinary extent to which knowledge from new fields has been drawn upon.

A number of key practitioners have independently, around the same time period, had significant influence upon these two trends. The first of these was apparently the American psychiatrist N.W. Ackerman, who in the early 1940's began with psychoanalytic therapy with children, then with the mother and child, and finally with the entire family. His book, The Psychodynamics of Family Life, published in 1950, is still widely cited today. Also in the '40's, work by D. Levy on maternal overprotection, the classic work of J. Bowby on institutionalized infants in Britain, F. Fromm-Reichman's concept of the "schizophrenogenic" mother, and emerging studies in the fields of biology and physiology, especially the work of M. Mahler on symbiosis, Cannon on homeostasis, and the enormously influential work of H. Selye on stress, all helped set the stage for a re-examination of schizophrenia after World War II that culminated in the "family" therapy of schizophrenics in the early '50's. The team of G. Bateson, a cultural anthropologist who described schismogenesis in primitive peoples; J.H. Weakland, a chemical engineer originally; and J. Haley, a student of communications at Palo Alto, California; all collaborated with the psychiatrists W. Fry and D.D. Jackson to examine the communications and interaction patterns in schizophrenics, and postulated that what was commonly called "schizophrenia" was actually the "normal" response to a pattern of interaction in the family. It was here that systems theory and cybernetics found their way into the theory and practice of family counseling.

Around the same time, L.C. Wynne was deriving an etiology of schizophrenia also localized to the "family" and its dynamics. And M. Bowen's use of the concepts of contagion and symbiosis also implicated the family in schizophrenia.

In 1957, the work of these pioneers was reported to the American Orthopsychiatric Association, and the dissemination of these ideas spread rapidly and widely into the professional schools, clinics, and private practices of a wide variety of practitioners.

The bibliography which follows covers a later period, mostly the 1970's to the present, and gives the reader a guide through the welter of developments in this period that have taken off from the early beginnings.

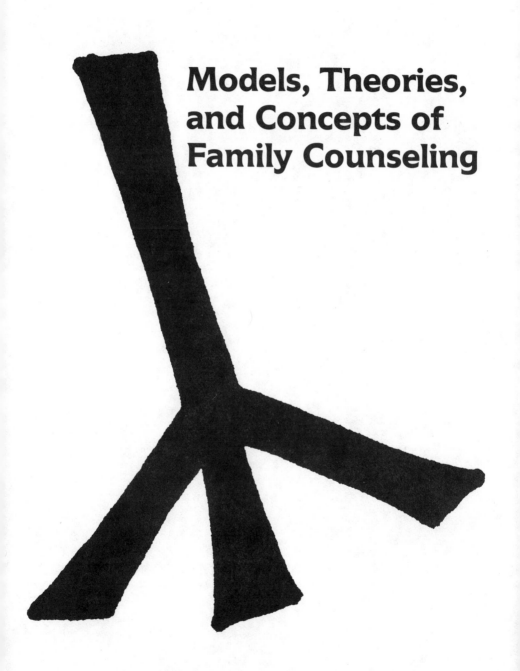

Models, Theories, and Concepts of Family Counseling

The citations contained in this section include seminal publications on family counseling evolving from the several historical streams which have infused the field; articles on key concepts which have been adapted in a variety of ways to practice; and works which attempt either to synthesize knowledge or to construct an integrated model of practice.

1* Apter, M.J., and Smith, K.C. *Psychological Reversals. Some New Perspectives on the Family and Family Communication. Family Therapy 6(2): 89-100, 1979.*

According to "reversal theory," certain motivational states function in pairs of opposites that are bistable; change from one state to its opposite in such a pari is a reversal. This paper discusses this theory and shows how certain family problems, including some problems that reach clinical proportions, can arise from incompatabilities among family members in terms of such states. Appropriate therapeutic procedures are suggested to deal with such cases.

---

2 Bagarozzi, Dennis A., and Wodarski, John S. *Behavioral Treatment of Marital Discord. Clinical Social Work Journal 6(2):135-154, 1978.*

Many techniques derived from various family therapies such as filial therapy, conjugal therapy, conjoint parent/ child therapy, conjoint marital therapy, and conjoint family therapy, have recently been incorporated into the practice, skills, and repertory of clinical social workers. Of these approaches, the behavioral view has a substantial pool of accumulated data to support its wide use in practice. However, virtually no detailed explanation of the behavioral view appears in the social work literature, thus hindering its application. To alleviate this deficiency, the

*The numbers in front of each bibliographic citation correspond to the numbers contained in the index that appears at the end of this book.

following topics are reviewed: basic philosophy, behavioral exchange and marital satisfaction, development of marital confict, clinical implications, clinical assessment, tools for intervention, and procedural guidelines for the treatment process.

---

3 Barnhill, Laurence R. *Healthy Family Systems.*
Family Coordinator 28(1):94-100, 1979.

From a review of the relevant writings of the major workers in the field, eight dimensions (e.g., individuation vs. enmeshment, flexibility vs. rigidity, and stability vs. disorganization) of health family functioning are isolated and discussed. These dimensions can be integrated as a mutually causal system, the "family health cycle." The different styles of leading family therapists can be seen as espousing different points of entry into the "family health cycle." The need for studying healthy families in family therapy training programs is discussed.

---

4 Barnhill, L.R., and Longo, D. *Fixation and Regression in the Family Life Cycle. Family Process 12(4):469-478, 1978.*

In spite of the obvious fact that families differ significantly depending upon their current stage in the life cycle, most of the family therapy literature focuses on intervening in ongoing family interaction without specific attention to the dimension of family development. This paper explores the utility of the family developmental view, using the concepts of fixation and regression in the family life cycle. These concepts were found to be relatively refined and quite pragmatic assessment devices that assist therapists in specifying developmental issues of the family.

---

5 Berenson, Gerald. *Attachment Theory, Object-Relations Theory, and Family Therapy. Family Therapy 3(3):183-195, 1976.*

The use of Bowlby's attachment theory and object relations theory as part of a general theory of family development

10

is discussed. Previous research on attachment and object relations, and clinical examples illustrating the use of this theory in a family therapy setting, are presented.

---

6 Berenson, Gerald, and White, Harvey, eds. *Annual Review of Family Therapy*. New York: Human Sciences Press, 1980.

This book presents a comprehensive overview of theoretical, research, and clinical developments of interest to all family therapists. It offers an array of therapeutic techniques and concepts which include psychodynamics, object relations, psychoanalysis, communications, and family systems theories. Particular attention is given to two critical issues in contemporary society--depression and divorce.

---

7 Bloch, Donald A. *Family Therapy, Group Therapy*. *International Journal of Group Psychotherapy* 26(3):289-299, 1976.

The author contends that meaningful differences exist between group and family therapy. In group therapy, as in individual therapy, the behavior of the individual is the target of treatment, whereas in family therapy efforts focus on changing the family system. The family is described as being a primary, natural, ongoing group, rather than as a constructed group.

---

8 Bowen, Murray. *Alcoholism as Viewed Through Family Systems Theory and Family Psychotherapy*. *Annals of the New York Academy of Sciences 233*: 115-122, April, 1974.

The author outlines the principles of family systems theory, in which alcoholism is conceptualized as a symptom of the larger family or social unit. Ways in which family or systems theory can be used to alleviate these problems are cited.

---

9 Brodkin, Adele M. Family Therapy: The Making of a Mental Health Movement. American Journal of Orthopsychiatry 50(1):4-17, 1980.

A historical account of the development of the family therapy movement is presented, stressing its multifaceted approach., Originally, family therapy grew out of treatments for schizophrenic children when it was found that family relationships were important factors in the etiology of schizophrenia. Thus, its focus was on helping the individual family member. In the 1960's, its emphasis shifted toward saving the institution of the nuclear family from attacks by the counterculture. The evolution of numerous types of therapy for the family is presented.

---

10 Ebert, Bruce. Homeostasis. Family Therapy 5(2):171-175, 1978.

Homeostasis is defined as it is used scientifically and in its explanatory usefulness to family therapy and human psychological behavior. The work of Cannon (1938), Jackson (1954, 1970), and Satir (1967, 1972, 1976) are discussed as they relate to the latter issue. It is suggested that homeostasis in families is basically an unconscious process, and the issue of group-centered determinism is raised. Serious problems in family homeostasis may arise when one member receives treatment, or when the system is highly resistant to change, perhaps due to fear of the unknown.

---

11 Ellis, Albert. Family Therapy: A Phenomenological and Active Directive Approach. Journal of Marriage and Family Counseling 4(2):43-50, 1978.

Because the most popular forms of family therapy--psychodynamic and systems-oriented therapy--appreciably fail to consider family members as individuals in their own right, a phenomenological-humanistic view of families who come for therapy would serve to correct this oversight. It is noted that the particular phenomenological view espoused by those who do client-centered family therapy, however, is too passive and neglects some of the realities of human disturbance. A "third force" in family therapy

12

is therefore outlined in this paper, which combines a phenomenological-humanistic approach with a highly active-directive attempt to help family members surrender their misperceptions of themselves and others and to make profound philosophic changes in their intrapersonal and interpersonal attitudes and behaviors.

12 Family Service Association of America. The Many Dimensions of Family Practice: Proceedings of the North American Symposium on Family Practice, November, 1978. New York: Family Service Association of America, 1980.

The 32 papers in this publication are intended to provide the individual practitioner in family practice with an accurate presentation of the ideas and methodologies currently extant in the field. Papers cover methods of service and intervention in areas like "The Non-Nuclear Family."

13 Fellner, Carl. The Use of Teaching Stories in Conjoint Family Therapy. Family Process 15(4): 427-431, 1976.

In this paper, a form of therapeutic communication called the teaching story is presented, which embodies a mixture of both the educational and the paradox, or the absurd.

14 Frager, Stuart. Multiple Family Therapy: A Literature Review. Family Therapy 5(2):105-120, 1978.

This article focuses on the various applications of multiple family therapy in inpatient and outpatient psychiatric settings and correctional institutions. Theoretical considerations are summarized, delineating the stages of therapy within sessions and throughout the course of treatment, and the curative factors involved. Personal qualities required of the multiple family therapist, and his/her function as a group leader and change agent, are discussed.

*15 Framo, James L.   Family Theory and Therapy.
American Psychologist 34(10):988-992, 1979.*

Whereas psychologists have traditionally focused on individuals, family system theory largely deals with what
happens between people, especially closely related ones.
Family system theory emphasizes contexts, particularly
the intimate context of the family as a powerful motivating
and organizing force in human behavior. This psychology
of intimate relationships provides a bridge between the
personal and the social. Family and marital therapy are
clinical applications of the system viewpoint that is creating a revolution in clinical practice. Psychopathology
is viewed as a consequence of relationship struggles
between intimates.

---

*16 Freeman, David S.   A Systems Approach to Family
Therapy. Family Therapy 3(1):61-73, 1976.*

Discusses the implications of using a general systems perspective in working with families. Using references to
the literature, a number of principles are delineated, and
their application in using systems ideas for diagnosis and
treatment is illustrated. It is concluded that converting
systems ideas into actual practice requires much effort,
but that the results are worthwhile.

---

*17 Goode, William.   Force and Violence in the Fam-
ily. Journal of Marriage and the Family, pp. 624-
636, November, 1971.*

Goode discusses the use of force in all social systems,
and particularly within the family. One section covers
violence within the family and discusses the roles of persons engaged in the violent action from an exchange
perspective.

---

*18 Gray, W., and Gray, L. R.   Systems Specifics in
"Break-In"--A Therapeutic Approach. International
Journal of Offender Therapy and Comparative
Criminology 21(1):31-40, 1977.*

"System specifics" is a form of general systems theory, developed for use in psychotherapy and counseling, that has proven effective in the treatment of juvenile delinquents, adult offenders, and neurotic patients.

---

19 Greenberg, G. S. The Family Interactional Perspective: A Study and Examination of the Work of Don D. Jackson. Family Process 16(4):385-412, 1977.

This article presents an overview of the primary contributions of the late Don D. Jackson. It analyzes and attempts to unify the central concepts of what was first referred to as "conjoint family therapy." Emphasis is upon the theoretical components leading to the development of a behaviorally oriented, nontransference, focused-treatment format, labeled by the author as "family interactional psychotherapy."

---

20 Grunebaum, H., and Chasin, R. Relabeling and Reframing Reconsidered: The Beneficial Effects of a Pathological Label. Family Process 17(4):449-455, 1978.

Traditional labeling theory usually contends that pathological labels contribute to pathology and that benign labels help alleviate it. However, it is likely that the role of pathological labels as the cause of pathology has been overstated and overgeneralized. Family therapists have probably over-used the practice of substituting a benign label for a pathological label ("relabeling"). In fact, there are many families in which a pathological label applied to one family member may have beneficial impact on the entire family system, including on that member.

---

21 Guerin, Philip J., ed. Family Therapy: Theory and Practice. New York: Gardner Press, 1976.

This text about family therapy presents 32 chapters on family therapy by psychiatrists, psychoanalysts, psychotherapists, and social workers.

---

*22 Gurman, Alan S., and Kniskern, David P.
Deterioration in Marital and Family Therapy:
Empirical, Clinical, and Conceptual Issues. Family Process 17(1):3-20, 1978.*

Recent empirical evidence is presented of deterioration
during both nonbehavioral and behavioral marital and
family therapy. While the frequency of patient worsening
in marital-family therapy does not appear to exceed that
previously found for individual psychotherapy, the acceptability of the evidence for negative effects in the treatment of systems may be greater than that which exists for
individual treatment.

---

*23 Gurman, Alan S., and Kniskern, David P. Tech-
nolatry, Methodolatry, and the Results of Family
Therapy. Family Process 17(3):275-281, 1978.*

Wells and Dezen's revisited results of research on the outcomes of nonbehavioral family therapy are themselves
revisited. While their conclusions are largely defensible
in terms of conventional criteria for research design and
for assessing change in psychotherapy, this article questions whether such standard criteria are sufficient for
studying the outcomes of family therapy.

---

*24 Gurman, Alan S., and Knudson, Roger M. Behav-
ioral Marriage Therapy: I. A Psychodynamic-
Systems Analysis and Critique. Family Process
17(2):121-138, 1978.*

After briefly summarizing the major theoretical premises
and treatment strategies of behavioral marriage therapy
(BMT), the authors identify and critically examine five
major clusters of implicit assumptions in BMT: "the
rational observing ego shall conquer all"; "behavior
should not mean, but be"; "what's sauce for the goose
is sauce for the gander"; "repression is good for your
marital mental health"; and "the folly of the therapist as
technician." The conceptual and clinical limitations of a
strictly or predominantly behavioral approach to couples
therapy are described, and BMT is reconsidered in the

light of object relations theory and communication theory perspectives on marital dysfunction and its treatment.

---

25 Gurman, Alan S., and Knudson, Roger M. Behavioral Marriage Therapy: IV. Take Two Aspirin
and Call Us in the Morning. Family Process
17(2):165-180, 1978.

The authors argue that Jacobson and Weiss' critique of the Gurman-Knudson and Gurman-Kniskern discussions of behavioral marriage therapy (BMT), while scholarly, derives from such a narrow conceptual set that, with only minor exceptions, Jacobson and Weiss have failed basically to comprehend the essence of the theoretical and logical criticisms of BMT. Moreover, a careful reanalysis of the research cited by Jacobson-Weiss as evidence for the effi-cacy of BMT reveals the strength of the empirical founda-tion of this approach to have been greatly exaggerated.

---

26 Haley, Jay. Changing Families: A Family Therapy Reader. New York: Grove and Stratton, 1971.

This collection brings together papers on family therapy which have been published in various journals over the years, along with several new articles not previously published. Although the focus of the collection is on therapy technique more than on family diagnosis or family dynamics, many authors emphasize the problems to be changed as well as the experiences involved with being a family therapist.

---

27 Haley, Jay. Problem-Solving Therapy: New
Strategies for Effective Family Therapy. San
Francisco: Jossey-Bass, 1976.

This book is directed at therapists who are interested in developing specific techniques and skills for solving human problems in the context of the family. Haley's concept of diagnosis is discussed, as well as the considerations to which each therapist must attend in each situation to develop strategies that will lead to solutions. Regarding

the question of how to train a good therapist, Haley pre-
scribes in-person supervision and a systematic examination of the outcomes of treatment.

---

28 Haley, Jay. *Uncommon Therapy: The Psychiatric Techniques of Milton H. Erickson, M.D.* New York: W.W. Norton, 1973.

Although the main focus of this book is on Erickson,
whose practice utilizes a blend of psychiatry, hypnosis,
and conditioning, Haley also presents his own ideas on
family therapy and practice.

---

29 Halleck, Seymour L. *Family Therapy and Social Change.* Social Casework 57(8):483-493, 1976.

The author discusses changing freedom, power, equality,
and responsibility in relation to functioning of family and
society. Family therapists can contribute to revision of
values which may be destructive. Individual freedom
must be limited to avoid oppressing the less powerful.

---

30 Heard, D.H. *From Object Relations to Attach-ment Theory: A Basis for Family Therapy.* British Journal of Medical Psychology 51(1):67-76, 1978.

Reasons are put forward for the choice of attachment
theory as a basis for family therapy and to suggest
hypotheses to investigate the quality and quantity of
intrafamilial social interaction and concomitant emotional
states. The family in family therapy is described in terms
of the interpersonal dynamic suggested by attachment
theory. The family is seen as a homeostatic system of
relationships between individuals at different stages of
development who share set goals aimed at terminating a
specific form of proximity-seeking attachment behavior and
at promoting exploratory behavior.

---

31 Hindman, Margaret. *Family Therapy in Alcohol-ism.* Alcohol Health and Research World 1(1):1-9, 1976.

The advantages of a family systems approach to treating alcoholism are detailed, and a summary of the theoretical underpinnings of the family therapy concept is given. Also, current research efforts in the field are summarized.

---

32 Hodgson, J.W., and Lewis, R.A. Pilgrim's Progress III: A Trend Analysis of Family Theory and Methodology. Family Process 18(2):163-173, 1979.

Exciting developments in family theory construction over the past few years demand a constant survey and evaluation of measurable progress. This paper documents some developmental trends that have taken place in family theory construction and its applications, as well as in the relation of theory to advances in methodology.

---

33 Hughes, Sally F., Berger, Michael, and Wright, Larry. The Family Life Cycle and Clinical Intervention. Journal of Marital and Family Therapy 4(4):33-40, 1978.

With an aim toward encouraging more precise identification and treatment of familial dysfunction, the authors suggest combining the principles of first- and second-order change with the concept of the family life cycle. Theoretical discussion is followed by clinical case examples.

---

34 James, Susan L. Family Therapy: A Comparison of Approaches. Bowie, Maryland: Robert J. Brady Company, 1980.

This book is a straightforward theoretical/clinical reference that ties together the multivaried strands of today's family therapy fabric. It examines and then cross-compares the similarities and differences of seven major theoretical approaches.

---

35 Janeksela, G.M. Mandatory Parental Involvement in the Treatment of Delinquent Youth. Juvenile and Family Court Journal 30(1):47-54, 1979.

An argument is presented for increasing parental responsibility in the treatment of juvenile behavior problems. Social and legal considerations related to mandatory parental involvement are evaluated. A legislative model for mandatory parental involvement in treatment is proposed in which family counseling and intensive supervision of family processes take place by a specially trained family crisis unit of the juvenile court.

---

36 Kaplan, Marvin L., and Kaplan, Netta R. *Individual and Family Growth: A Gestalt Approach. Family Process 17(2):195-205, 1978.*

Describes Gestalt therapy as a comprehensive framework of theory and techniques for experiential family therapy. Like other experientially oriented therapies, it is systems-oriented, immediate-experience-oriented, and affect-oriented. Unlike others, this method regards the client system's emergent processes as the central focus, and it emphasizes that growth occurs as the family and its members are helped to greater self-awareness and responsibility for their own functioning.

---

37 Keeney, B.P. *Ecosystemic Epistemology: An Alternative Paradigm for Diagnosis. Family Process 18(2):117-129, 1979.*

An alternative paradigm for diagnosis based on cybernetics, ecology, and systems theory is proposed. This paradigm, termed "ecosystemic epistemology," suggests that diagnosis focus on knowing problematic situations in an ecological and systemic way. Theoretical statements concerning this approach are delineated with specific references to prominent family therapists.

---

38 Klein, N.C., and Parsons, E.V. *Impact of Family Systems Intervention on Recidivism and Sibling Delinquency--A Model of Primary Prevention and Program Evaluation. Journal of Consulting and Clinical Psychology 45(3):469-474, 1977.*

A program evaluation model, focusing on the tertiary, secondary, and primary prevention effects of intervention, is described as it applies to an intervention program for delinquents that emphasizes family interaction.

---

39 Langsford, Richard. *Understanding the Role of Extrafamilial Social Forces in Family Treatment: A Critique of Family Therapy*. Family Therapy 5(1):73-80, 1978.

The field of family therapy has tended to isolate the family from its social, economic, and political environment, which is detrimental to both understanding and treating troubled families. While family therapists frequently acknowledge the plight of the modern nuclear family, this awareness is not integrated into either theory or practice.

---

40 Langsley, Donald G. *Three Models of Family Therapy: Prevention, Crisis Treatment, or Rehabilitation*. Journal of Clinical Psychiatry 39(11):792-796, 1978.

This article describes models of intervention at a family level as preventive, crisis intervention, or rehabilitative. The preventive model suggests that certain stresses produce family disorganization, and individual family members may regress to symptoms of disease. Family dysfunction could be avoided through identification of high-risk groups and intervention at developmental milestones. The data on early intervention with children has produced the most promising results. Crisis intervention, the second model, suggests that early identification and prompt intervention may avoid the development of more serious disorganization. The rehabilitation model is focused on changing long-term patterns of maladaptive behavior. It includes the home-ostasis model, the conflict resolution model, and other approaches to long-term family therapy.

---

41 Levande, Diane I. *Family Theory as a Necessary Component of Family Therapy*. Social Casework 57(5):291-295, 1976.

The author outlines three contemporary approaches to the study of the family and their implications for family intervention. The structure-functional framework approach views the family as the smallest social system in transaction with the external environment. The health of the system is measured by its ability to maintain boundaries and regain equilibrium when stress is induced by other social systems. This theory suggests therapeutic intervention which strengthens the family's boundary-maintaining ability and reduces destructive outside influences. The interactional framework approach emphasizes the interaction of persons and subsystems within the family; therapy focuses on this internal functioning. The developmental framework approach stresses stages and tasks in the family life cycle; therapists focus on prevention and family change.

---

42 Levant, Ronald F. *Client-Centered Approaches to Working with the Family: An Overview of New Developments in Therapeutic, Educational, and Preventive Methods. American Journal of Family Therapy 6(1):31-44, 1978.*

An overview of recently developed, client-centered helping programs for the family is given. These programs include a client-centered form of family therapy and three types of family educational programs.

---

43 Levant, Ronald F. *Family Therapy: A Client-Centered Perspective. Journal of Marriage and Family Counseling 4(2):35-42, 1978.*

The author critiques therapist-directed approaches to family therapy in the light of research findings on therapist variables (empathy, warmth, genuineness) associated with positive outcomes in psychotherapy. Two polar opposite positions in family therapy--psychodynamic and family systems--are also examined and found to have much in common. The two approaches are based on a pessimistic view of the family, which is seen as an intractable unit, resistant to its own growth. Finally, an alternative, phenomenological view of the family is developed, which more optimistically assumes the family to be motivated for

enhancement and growth. A client-centered approach
to family therapy is described.

---

*44 Luban-Plozza, B.   Psychosomatic Practice and
the Concept of Family Confrontation as Therapeuti-
cal Method.   Psychotherapy and Psychosomatics
31(4):301-306, 1979.*

Psychosocial dynamics within the family are discussed. It
is one of the special tasks of the general practitioner to
be alert to the first signs of emotional disturbances; he
or she has to acquire a valid picture of the family unit,
with its physical and psychological strengths and short-
comings. In the long run, continued flight from pressure
of vital issues can lead to family neurosis. The sick person is then not really the carrier of disease in the traditional sense of germ or genetic causation; he is only a
"symptom" of a much more widely encompassing disease
unit that has grasped a social cell like the family.

---

*45 Minuchin, Salvador.   Families and Family Ther-
apy.   Cambridge, Massachusetts: Harvard University Press, 1974.*

Minuchin presents a conceptual framework for understanding the family ecologically, in its internal and external transactions. A study of two well-functioning families
in two different cultures is used to illustrate his point of
view. Minuchin's therapeutic approach is akin to a life
model of practice in which the family is viewed develop-
mentally; it faces particular tasks at particular stages of
transition and interacts with demands for change posed by
the social and cultural context. These demands, together
with the family's transactional patterns, its flexibility and
sensitivity, its social context, and its use of symptoms for
system maintenances, form the basis for assessment,
mutual goal-setting, and helping procedures.

---

*46 Mostwin, Danuta.   Social Dimension of Family
Treatment.   Washington, D.C.:   National Association of Social Workers, 1980.*

The author has devised the use of a treatment model called Short-Term Multidimensional Family Intervention. Based on the family life space concept, the model has proved especially useful with less verbal families and their children. Emphasis is placed on the importance of cultural factors in treatment. The model is especially useful when working with families from minority and ethnic groups.

---

47 Olson, D.H., Sprenkle, D.H., and Russell, C.S. Circumplex Model of Marital and Family System: I. Cohesion and Adaptability Dimensions, Family Types, and Clinical Applications. Family Process 18(1):3-28, 1979.

The conceptual clustering of numerous concepts from family therapy and other social science fields reveals two significant dimensions of family behavior--cohesion and adaptability. These two dimensions are placed into a circumplex model that is used to identify 16 types of marital and family systems.

---

48 Orten, James D. Organizing Concepts in Family Therapy. American Journal of Family Therapy 6(1):9-16, 1978.

The author argues that the number of approaches to family therapy represents a variety of theoretical perspectives and assumptions about human behavior. Comparisons of real differences and similarities are difficult because each approach has, to some extent, a unique language. This article describes a model that goes beyond semantics and facilitates meaningful comparison of different versions of family therapy.

---

49 Perez, Joseph F. Family Counseling. New York: Van Nostrand, Reinhold, 1979.

This comprehensive overview of the theory and techniques of family counseling focuses on family interaction as the primary cause of the individual emotional problems. The book describes the concepts of emotional homeostasis, the identified patient, and dyads and triads within the family structure, providing a thorough explanation of the theoretical basis of the systems approach.

50 *Riess, Bernard F. Family Therapy as Seen by a Group Therapist. International Journal of Group Psychotherapy 26(3):301-309, 1976.*

The author analyzes similarities and differences between group and family therapy from the viewpoint of Freudian psychoanalytically based group therapy, arguing that the two are widely varying approaches to widely divergent problems. Differences in goals, evaluations, and the factors influencing outcomes are discussed.

51 *Rueveni, Uri. Networking Families in Crisis: Intervention Strategies with Families and Social Networks. New York: Human Sciences Press, 1979.*

The technique of mobilizing the extended system of family, relatives, friends, and neighbors for helping a family during times of emotional crisis is described. Specific issues treated include techniques used for mobilizing the extended social system, goals of intervention, training the network intervention team, and the role of the family therapist as a system interventionist.

52 *Scheflen, A. E. Susan Smiled: On Examplation in Family Therapy. Family Process 17(1):59-78, 1978.*

The contemporary psychotherapist is exposed to a variety of conceptual models and paradigms. These are usually presented as opposing truths in different doctrinal schools, but actually they are all valid from one point of view or another. And, accordingly, they are all tactically useful at some point or another.

53 *Shapiro, R. J. A Family Therapy Approach to Alcoholism. Journal of Marriage and Family Counseling 3(4):71-78, 1977.*

A family therapy approach to alcoholism is proposed, based on known characteristics of family systems and clinical experiences. Specific strategies are described that can enhance treatment success by reducing resistances and maximizing changes in dysfunctional family interaction patterns. Since the relationship between the spouses may perpetuate the need for alcohol, the major focus in therapy is on understanding and changing the marital relationship.

---

54 Skynner, A.C. *Systems of Family and Marital Psychotherapy.* New York: Brunner/Mazel, 1976.

A comprehensive British contribution to the subject, integrating theory and practice.

---

55 Soper, Patricia G., and Labate, Lucian. *Paradox as a Therapeutic Technique: A Review.* American Journal of Family Therapy 5(1):10-21, 1977.

This article discusses the nature of paradox as a therapeutic intervention from a historical and theoretical perspective. Included is a review of types of paradoxical interventions, as well as a brief review of related approaches with heavy paradoxical overtones. Major emphasis is placed on the use of paradox in family therapy through relevant individual approaches such as paradoxical intention and hypnosis.

---

56 Spiegel, Renee, and Mock, William L. *A Model for a Family Systems Theory Approach to Prevention and Treatment of Alcohol Abusing Youth.* Cleveland, Ohio: Alcoholism Services of Cleveland, 1978.

The authors present a family systems theory approach to treatment of alcohol-abusing youth. The various components of the model, special issues involved in its implementation, and benefits derived from its use are detailed.

---

57 Spitz, Henry I. *Group Approaches to Treating Marital Problems. Psychiatric Annals 9(6):50-70, 1979.*

Prevention and treatment of marital problems have been enhanced by the development of group and family therapy practice and research. The central factors that contribute to a theoretical and practical understanding of these techniques are highlighted.

---

58 Sprey, Jetse. *The Family as a System in Conflict. Journal of Marriage and the Family 31:699-706, 1969.*

The author proposes an alternate to the equilibrium-consensus theory of familial interaction. He argues that a conflict theory is a more fruitful theoretical approach. A major implication is that familial harmony be considered a problematic rather than a normal state of affairs. This is a highly theoretical discussion.

---

59 Sprey, Jetse. *On the Management of Conflict in Families. Journal of Marriage and the Family (11):722-731, 1971.*

The author attempts to apply the conflict approach to a study of familial process. He looks at the concepts of bonding, aggression, appeasement, and threat. The extramarital aspects of conflict management also are discussed. This paper offers a conceptual view of conflict management in families.

---

60 Stanton, M.D., et al. *Heroin Addiction as a Family Phenomenon: A New Conceptual Model. American Journal of Drug and Alcohol Abuse 5(2):125-150, 1978.*

The chronic relapsing nature of heroin addiction can be explained from a family systems viewpoint. The addiction cycle is part of a family pattern involving a complex homeostatic system of interlocking feedback mechanisms. These

serve to maintain the addiction and consequently the overall family stability while the family becomes stuck at a
particular developmental stage.

---

*61 Strelnick, A.H.   Multiple Family Group Therapy:
A Review of the Literature.   Family Process
16(3):307-325, 1977.*

Historical, descriptive, and evaluative information on
Multiple Family Group Therapy (MFGT) are brought
together in this review of the literature. Separate consideration is given to the origin of MFGT in the inter-
section of family and group therapies, its goals and
dominant themes, its use in a variety of settings, its
specific techniques, the process of group development in
individual and ongoing meetings, and the parallels of
MFGT in other family and group work.

---

*62 Taylor, R.B.   Family Behavior Modification.
American Family Physician 19(3):176-181, 1979.*

Behavior modification has been effective in dealing with
problems in individual patients. The adaptation of behavior modification techniques to the family unit can help to
lessen some harmful consequences of adverse human
behavior. A formal written contract, involving all family
members and the physician, is useful.

---

*63 Wells, R.A., and Dezen, A.E.   Ideologies, Idols
(and Graven Images?):   Rejoinder to Gurman and
Kniskern.   Family Process 17(3):283-286, 1978.*

Three major issues raised in Gurman and Kniskern's
commentary are discussed. These are: the suitability
of established research design criteria for studying the
outcome of family therapy; the impact of therapist relationship factors on therapy outcome; and the place of concrete
or objective change measures in psychotherapy outcome
research. Areas of agreement and disagreement with
Gurman and Kniskern's observations are identified.

---

*64 Zuk, Gerald H. Family Therapy: Clinical Hodge-
podge or Clinical Science. Journal of Marriage
and Family Counseling 2(2):299-303, 1976.*

The author summarizes his views regarding family therapy. Topics covered included general propositions, the
therapist's role, the values expressed by therapist and
families, pathogenic family processes, types and goals of
the family therapy, phases of therapy, and limitations and
contraindications of such therapy. Because critics are
saying that family therapy is a hodgepodge of theories
and techniques, other therapists claiming an integrated
viewpoint are obligated to provide similar summaries in
simple terms that invite rigorous evaluation.

Applications
and the Practice
of Family Counseling

The largest number of publications about family counseling to come out in recent years has been in the area of the application and practice of counseling. Articles and chapters of books on topics such as counseling or therapy techniques, cross-cultural factors, adaptations of family counseling to a variety of settings and with a wide variety of target populations, assessing families, stages of treatment, traditional psychodynamic concepts applied to families--in short, a bewildering and bright array of a predominantly anecdotal and clinical nature--have all been the subject of written works. In large part, the publications cited here serve as the repository of practical knowledge on family counseling.

---

65 Ablon, Joan. *Family Behavior and Alcoholism.* In: *Cross-Cultural Approaches to the Study of Alcohol.* Paris: Mouton, 1976.

The literature on alcoholism and the family is reviewed, with emphasis on the wife of the alcoholic and interactions within the alcoholic marriage. The types of adaptation of the total family to stress caused by the existence of alcoholism in the household are also discussed.

---

66 Alexander, J. F., et al. *Systems-Behavioral Intervention with Families of Delinquents--Therapist Characteristics: Family Behavior and Outcome.* Journal of Consulting and Clinical Psychology 44(4):656-664, 1976.

A clinical setting was used to evaluate therapist characteristics, therapist progress, and family process in a short-term systems behavioral model of family intervention.

---

67 Anderson, L. M. *Character-Disordered Family--A Community Treatment Model for Family Sexual Abuse.* American Journal of Orthopsychiatry 29(3):436-445, 1979.

A collaborative approach to treating sexually abusive families is described in which such families are viewed as analogous to "character-disordered" individuals; family and marital therapy is provided.

---

68 Baither, Richard C. Family Therapy with Adolescent Drug Abusers: A Review. Journal of Drug Education 8(4):337-343, 1978.

A brief review of the literature is presented, covering such topics as treatment approaches, processes, goals, and programs. Reasons are given for treating the family of the adolescent drug abuser.

---

69 Balmer, Jared U., et al. High Impact Family Treatment--A Progress Report. Juvenile and Family Court Journal 30(1):3-7, 1979.

High impact family treatment, a form of therapy involving multiple therapists over a 2-day period for families of juvenile delinquents, is examined as a way of reducing recidivism, especially among status offenders.

---

70 Balmer, Jared U., Becvar, Raphael J., and Hinckley, Mark. Patterns of Redundancy in Marriage and Family Systems. Family Therapy 4(2):113-119, 1977.

This article discusses three redundant pathological behavior patterns found in marriage and family systems. By describing these patterns and comparing them with others, implications for psychotherapeutic intervention are developed.

---

71 Bank, Stephen, and Kahn, Michael D. Sisterhood-Brotherhood is Powerful: Sibling Sub-Systems and Family Therapy. In: Annual Progress in Child Psychiatry and Child Development, 1976.

This volume explores situations where siblings have profound influence on one another. Direct work with siblings provides the therapist with more options and a greater leverage in producing change for siblings, as well as for other family members.

---

72 Barash, Dorothy A. *Dynamics of the Pathological Family System.* Perspectives in Psychiatric Care 17(1):17-25, 1979.

Dynamics of the pathological family system are linked to the influence they may have on the growth and development of the individual within the family system. It is shown how family therapy can be effective when trying to change maladaptive family behavior patterns.

---

73 Baron, R. *Probation Officers, Family Crisis Counseling, and Juvenile Diversion, Parts 1 and 2.* Ann Arbor, Michigan: University Microfilms, 1977.

Use of short-term family crisis counseling for noncriminal juvenile delinquents and details of the operation of such a program in California are explored. This thesis includes a training manual.

---

74 Barton, Cole, and Alexander, James. *Therapists' Skills as Determinants of Effective Systems-Behavioral Family Therapy.* American Journal of Family Therapy 5(2):11-19, 1971.

Many problematic aspects of family therapy have been neglected by a behavioral family interventional focus on treatment technology, at the expense of ignoring critical aspects of family interaction and the idiographic characteristics of therapists as agents of service delivery. Preliminary empirical support is used to illustrate the intuitive assumption that a therapist's interpersonal style is critically related to effective family behavior change.

---

75 Bates, Paul. *The Search for Reinforcers to Training and Maintaining Effective Parent Behaviors. Rehabilitation Literature 39(9):291-295, 1977.*

Discusses techniques available to the parent trainer that utilize behavioral principles to teach behavioral principles. Reinforcers for maintenance of behavior change include arrangements for family members to reinforce each other (dinner out for mother, extra allowance for siblings), peer programing, and instruction in self-monitoring.

---

76 Battegay, R. *Psychotherapy of Drug Dependents and Alcoholics. In: Drug Dependence: Current Problems and Issues, edited by M.M. Glatt. Baltimore: University Park Press, 1977.*

The author presents a detailed review of therapeutic techniques, including individual psychotherapy (supportive, analytical, hypnosis, and behavioral therapy) and psychotherapies in which the patient is seen in a social context (group psychotherapy, family therapy, therapeutic community, and community therapy).

---

77 Beal, Edward W. *Use of the Extended Family in the Treatment of Multiple Personality. American Journal of Psychiatry 135(5):539-542, 1978.*

This article describes a female patient with the diagnosis of multiple personality who was treated by several therapists with different theoretical perspectives, including psychoanalysis and family systems therapy. These approaches to the patient's illness are compared, a new methodology of treatment is reported, and the impact of different ways of thinking about the patient is discussed.

---

78 Beck, Henry W. *Dream Analysis in Family Therapy. Clinical Social Work Journal 5(1):53-57, 1977.*

Theoretical and practical aspects of dream analysis in family therapy are explored with case examples. The dream is considered to be disguised communication, and it is used to aid in diagnosis and treatment by exploring the unconscious elements of family life. The dream is shown to be of special value with families that block communication or only appear to be cooperative. Deciphering the dream helps to open new possibilities of communication.

---

79 Beck, Michael. *Family Members' Perceptions and Use of Time: An Element in Family Treatment. Family Therapy 6(1):5-10, 1979.*

In families with significant psychopathology, the flow of time seems to stop, thus preventing constructive change. This problem is most acute when one parent has a strong wish not to grow up--usually, the mother fearing the loss of her physical attractiveness. The therapist must provide a relationship through which change can take place and halted family time can start to progress again.

---

80 Beck, Michael. *Family Therapy as Reciprocal Emotional Induction. Family Therapy 4(2):151-161, 1977.*

This article discusses the psychological inductions that occur between the patient, the therapist, and others who are important in the treatment. An extensive case history demonstrates that all family members, whether physically present or not, are influenced by the treatment. The ways in which this occurs are illustrated.

---

81 Bell, John E. *Family in Medical and Psychiatric Treatment: Selected Clinical Approaches. Journal of Operational Psychiatry 8(1):57-65, 1977.*

The author sees family therapy as a problem-solving process, in which the family therapist serves as a group leader and the therapy follows a sequence of stages similar to models for small-group behavior. The stages are labeled as initiation, testing, struggling for power, settling on a common task, struggles toward completion of the common task, completion of the task, and separating from therapy.

---

82 Benningfield, Anna B. *Multiple Family Therapy Systems. Journal of Marriage and Family Counseling 4(2):25-34, 1978.*

Multiple family therapy (MFT) is described as a treatment method which includes several families in a series of sessions with the therapist(s). A brief historical description of MFT is included, as well as reports of MFT groups found in the literature.

---

83 Bentovim, A. *Therapeutic Systems and Settings in the Treatment of Child Abuse. In: Challenge of Child Abuse. London: Academic Press, 1977.*

Therapeutic systems and settings in the treatment of child abuse are discussed through the clinical experiences of a family undergoing therapy.

---

84 Bentovim, Arnon, and Kinston, Warren. *Brief Focal Family Therapy When the Child Is the Referred Patient: I. Clinical. Journal of Child Psychology and Psychiatry and Allied Disciplines 19(1):1-12, 1978.*

The development of a method to carry out time-limited focused therapy with families is described. Two case examples with different psychopathology and family pathology are provided to demonstrate the process of formulation of dynamic hypotheses, the development of operational plans for therapists, and the changes in the family with therapy.

---

85 Berenson, David. *A Family Approach to Alcoholism. Psychiatric Opinion 13(1):33-38, 1976.*

A theoretical approach and techniques are described for working with couples who enter therapy with alcohol already identified as a significant problem. Based on

Bowen's family systems theory, the first phase of treatment emphasizes history-taking, cooling-off and distancing, involvement of family members in therapy, and assisting the alcoholic to stop drinking. In the second phase of treatment, the therapist reduces the emotional distancing, facilitates communication, and provides techniques to handle other problems, such as anger, intimacy, or sexual dissonance.

---

86 Berenson, David. Therapists' Relationship with Couples with an Alcoholic Member. In: Family Therapy of Drug and Alcohol Abuse. New York: Gardner Press, 1979.

An overview of an approach to alcohol problems is presented that integrates Bowen's family systems theory with Alcoholics Anonymous and Al-Anon concepts.

---

87 Berkowitz, D.A. On the Reclaiming of Denied Affects in Family Therapy. Family Process 16(4):495-501, 1977.

A central developmental task of the family is to help its members develop the capacity to cope with the grief attendant on separation and loss. Excerpts from conjoint family therapy are presented to illustrate the therapeutic interventions made in assisting a family to acknowledge denied grief over the separation of one of its members along with unspoken tender feelings within the family.

---

88 Bernal, G., and Baker, J. Toward a Metacommunicational Framework of Couple Interactions. Family Process 18(3):293-302, 1979.

A multi-level, metacommunicational framework to understand couple interactions is presented. Five interactional levels are defined following a mode of abstraction that parallels the theory of logical types; case examples are offered of couples interacting at each of the levels. The clinical implications of the framework, as a metaphor for understanding transactional processes, are discussed, with an emphasis on the pragmatics of working with punctuational differences, developing therapeutic strategies, measuring progress, and setting goals for therapy with couples.

---

89 Blumberg, Marvin L. Collateral Therapy for the Abused Child and the Problem Parent. American Journal of Psychotherapy 33(3):339-353, 1979.

A therapeutic approach to the psychopathology of child abuse must employ a holistic view of the family in crisis. The psychopathic personality of the parent with an abusive diathesis, later repeated in the child, is acquired in childhood when he or she is maltreated and not adequately nurtured and parented.

---

90 Bonnefil, Margaret C. Therapist, Save My Child: A Family Crisis Case. Clinical Social Work Journal 7(1):6-14, 1979.

The author describes five sessions with a mother and her 15-year-old daughter who was suddenly refusing to attend school. They were an insecure and inhibited pair in an intensely dependent relationship involving much ambivalence on both sides. Not only was the immediate school problem resolved, but the clients developed some awareness of their own underlying conflicts related to the developmental phase of the family and of how their ways of handling these conflicts affected one another.

---

91 Boyd, J.H. The Interaction of Family Therapy and Psychodynamic Individual Therapy in an Inpatient Setting. Psychiatry 42(2):99-111, 1979.

Although individual psychotherapy is an established treatment modality in psychoanalytically oriented hospitals, family therapy is a relative newcomer. Some authors have begun to try to build bridges between the two fields on the level of theory, but almost none has reported on the interaction between the two treatment modalities on a pragmatic level when they are conducted simultaneously.

---

*92 Braiman, Susan G.   The Establishment of a
Therapeutic Alliance with Parents of Psychiatric-
ally Hospitalized Children.   Social Work in Health
Care 3(1):19-27, 1977.*

In response to the increased use of family therapy as an
adjunct to the treatment of emotionally disturbed children,
hospital-based social workers are impelled to explore the
initial barriers to effective parental involvement. As the
preconditions for successful, family-oriented treatment are
examined, the changes for creative and skillful social work
are maximized.

---

*93 Breunlin, Douglas C., and Southgate, Pam.   An
Interactional Approach to Dysfunctional Silencing
in Family Therapy.   Family Process 17(2):207-216,
1978.*

The authors present an interactional approach to the problem of dysfunctional silencing in family therapy. Silencing is classified as dysfunctional if it satisfies two conditions: it occurs repeatedly and independently of content,
and it functions as negative feedback that limits change in
the family system. Dysfunctional silencing is defined as
those efforts of one or more family members to limit change
by repeatedly blocking the communication of another family
member, who in turn colludes by tacitly agreeing to remain
silent.

---

*94 Bullock, D., and Thompson, B.   Guidelines for
Family Interviewing and Brief Therapy by the Family Physician.   Journal of Family Practice 9(5):
837-841, 1979.*

Psychosomatic and behavioral problems are commonly seen
in the practice of family medicine. If these problems are
viewed as difficulties with family interaction, rather than
as difficulties of an individual family member, intervention
may be more successful. Treatment of families with problems involves interviewing the family unit, identifying
and altering dysfunctional behavioral patterns within the

family which serve to maintain the problem, and making selected referrals to experienced family therapists.

---

95 Bullock, Dorothy, and Kobayashi, Ken. The Use of Live Consultation in Family Therapy. Family Therapy 5(3):245-250, 1978.

This article presents guidelines for therapists who are beginning to use the live consultation model. In live consultation, a therapist and consultant who are peers in approach, knowledge, and skills collaborate to increase family motivation, decrease resistance, and speed up therapy. The consultant views the session from behind a one-way mirror to intervene at strategic moments. Points of intervention and pitfalls are described.

---

96 Burquest, G. Severe Female Delinquency--When to Involve the Family in Treatment. In: Adolescent Psychiatry, Volume 7. Chicago: University of Chicago Press, 1979.

Presents guidelines by which therapists can decide how and when to involve the family in the treatment of adolescent female delinquents.

---

97 Butehorn, Loretta. A Plan for Identifying Priorities in Treating Multiproblem Families. Child Welfare 57(6):365-372, 1978.

A conceptual framework is presented for working with problem-ridden, crisis-prone families. The family structure and the interactions/processes that attempt to meet the needs of family members are viewed as the key components of the framework. The structure of the family is assessed in four areas--family self-concept, roles, family rules, and family boundaries. Communicating, parenting, and coping are seen as the essential processes to be evaluated for their effectiveness in meeting the needs of the family. Methods of gathering data in each of these areas are suggested.

42

*98 Cadogan, Donald A. Marital Group Therapy in
Alcoholism Treatment. In: Family Therapy of Drug
and Alcohol Abuse. New York: Gardner Press,
1979.*

Marital group therapy, which includes the spouse of the
alcoholic in the treatment of alcoholism, is described.
Clinical and experiential evidence support the view that
marital group therapy is an effective form of treatment for
alcoholism.

---

*99 Cameron, Lyle. St. Croix: An Outpatient Fam-
ily Treatment Approach. Alcohol Health and
Research World 3(4):16-17, 1979.*

The success of the St. Croix program in outpatient counseling and family therapy is attributed to having trained
staff and utilizing the Alcoholics Anonymous philosophy.

---

*100 Canino, Ian A., and Canino, Glorisa. Impact
of Stress on the Puerto Rican Family: Treatment
Considerations. American Journal of Orthopsychiatry 50(3):535-540, 1980.*

The impact of stress, due to migration and poverty, on
the family structure of the low-income Puerto Rican family
is discussed. The ecostructural family therapy approach
is suggested as a therapeutic modality for this high-risk
group. Treatment pitfalls and effective therapeutic techniques are illustrated.

---

*101 Carter, E.A. Generation After Generation: The
Long-Term Treatment of an Irish Family with Wide-
spread Alcoholism Over Multiple Generations. In:
Family Therapy, Full Length Case Studies. New
York: Gardner Press, 1977.*

Describes family counseling from 1974 to 1976 of a husband
and a wife, both from large Irish families containing many
heavy drinkers.

---

102 Chamow, Larry. *A Functional Approach to Family Assessment.* Family Therapy 2(3):259-268, 1975.

A method is described for organizing data which focuses on the strengths, rather than on the pathologies, revealed in family interviews as an aid in planning treatment goals and strategy. Twelve types of typical family characteristics are defined and illustrated by a case example.

---

103 Clarkin, J. E., Frances, A. J., and Moodie, J. L. *Selection Criteria for Family Therapy.* Family Process 18(4):391-403, 1979.

The patient-selection criteria for most modalities of psychotherapy have not yet been clearly articulated. This paper presents a decision-tree model outlining the factors that incline a clinician to perform a family evaluation, then to decide upon family treatment instead of another form of therapy, and finally to settle upon the particular duration and intensity of family treatment. This article compiles screening criteria, based on research and clinical opinion, to be applied in the utilization review of the decisions made at each of these steps.

---

104 Cohn, Cal K., and Talmadge, John M. *Extended Family Presents.* Family Therapy 3(3):235-244, 1976.

The impact of the extended family on the nuclear family is discussed. Previous studies and clinical case reports illustrating this impact are presented. Techniques of dealing with this family therapy situation are also discussed.

---

105 Coleman, Sandra B. *Family as a Vehicle for Confronting Drug/Alcohol Crisis.* Eagleville, Pennsylvania: 1978.

In this discussion of family involvement in addiction and its treatment, drug and alcohol problems are described as intrinsically representing crises, with death as a possible consequence. The author outlines a family systems approach to treatment.

---

106 *Constantine, Larry L. Family Sculpture and Relationship Mapping Techniques. Journal of Marriage and Family Counseling 4(2)13-23, 1978.*

Presents an overview of space and action techniques used in marriage and family therapy. It is pointed out that family sculpture and a variety of closely related techniques have gained wide acceptance by counselors, therapists, and educators.

---

107 *Cormont, Louis S., and Stream, Herbert S. The Practice of Conjoint Therapy. New York: Human Sciences Press, 1978.*

This book describes the use of psychoanalytically oriented individual and group therapy done with two different therapists. The method involves the conscious induction and deliberate manipulation of the intense multiple transferences aroused by such treatment.

---

108 *Cutler, D.L., and Madore, E. Community-Family Network Therapy in a Rural Setting. Community Mental Health Journal 16(2):144-155, 1980.*

A model of family intervention with extended family members and significant community agency personnel is presented in an attempt to deal with the total social network surrounding a seriously dysfunctional family. Described is how this approach adapts itself well to a rural setting and seems to encompass most if not all of the significant helping systems in the family social sphere. The authors believe that this approach has a facilitating effect to increase the functionality of already-existing natural social systems on which the family are already quite dependent, but which prior to the network sessions were largely non-functional.

---

109 *Davis, Donald I.* *Alcoholics Anonymous and*
Family Therapy. *Journal of Marital and Family*
Therapy 5:65-73, 1980.

The author focuses on ways in which advances in the
treatment of alcoholism contributed by family therapy have
been used in a manner that complement rather than detract
from the contributions of Alcoholics Anonymous, Al-Anon,
and Alateen. An historical review of family therapy is
presented.

---

110 *David, Donald I.* *Family Therapy for the Drug*
User: *Conceptual and Practical Considerations.*
Drug Forum 6(3):197-205, 1977-78.

A model of addiction is considered that supposes that the
interpersonal system or family into which the individual is
born has some investment in placing and keeping the individual in a particular role. The model provides understanding of the cyclic nature of addiction (detoxification
and readdiction). An effective treatment program, therefore, must deal with the systems that serve to maintain
the addiction, break the cycle, and provide the family
with the experience of functioning without a drug-dependent member.

---

111 *Davis, Donald I., and Steinglass, Peter.*
Therapeutic Strategies in Conjoint Hospitalization
for the Treatment of Alcoholism. *In:* *Family*
Therapy of Drug and Alcohol Abuse. *New York:*
Gardner Press, 1979.

Special methods are described in which conjoint hospitalization was used to therapeutic advantage in alcoholism
treatment. The therapy was conducted during a 10-day
experience with conjoint hospitalization of husbands and
wives, as an adjunct to therapy for alcoholism in one or
both spouses.

---

112 *Dayringer, R.* *Family Therapy Techniques for*
the Family Physician. *Journal of Family Practice*
6(2):303-307, 1978.

Family physicians have routinely recognized problem families within their practice. Skills and techniques are suggested in this article for introducing changes within a
family system.

---

113 DeShazer, Steve. *Brief Therapy with Couples.*
American Journal of Family Therapy 6(1):17-30,
1978.

The author presents a model of brief therapy with couples
that is based on "balance therapy." This model allows
the therapist to develop a cognitive map of the relationship
through the use of graphs, and then to plan a specific
step-by-step approach to the therapy of a particular couple. The couple is viewed as an interlocking system of
interdependent relationships.

---

114 DeShazer, Steve. *The Optimist-Pessimist Technique. Family Therapy 4(2):93-100, 1977.*

A therapeutic method labeled the optimist-pessimist technique was used in working with families that are rigidly
stuck in their problems and interactions. The technique
is illustrated by an actual case. Practical implications for
the family therapist are offered.

---

115 Diguiseppe, Ray, and Wilner, Stefanie R. *An
Eclectic View of Family Therapy: When Is Family
Therapy the Treatment of Choice? When Is It Not?
Journal of Clinical Child Psychology 9(1):70-72,
1980.*

Family therapy has grown considerably and is often the
treatment of choice for childhood disorders. Despite its
effectiveness, there are cases where family therapy is
ineffective. Based on clinical experience, indications of
family therapy are hypothesized. Also, suggestions for
combining family therapy with other modalities are provided.

---

116 Dinaburg, Daniel, Glick, Ira D., and
Feigenbaum, Elliot. *Marital Therapy of Women
Alcoholics*. Journal of Studies on Alcohol 38(7):
1247-1258, 1977.

A detailed case study of a 51-year old alcoholic housewife
recounts the failure of an attempt at family therapy. While
no claims to generalization are to be induced from this particular instance, it is inferred that marital therapy might
not warrant the optimistic assertions of its protagonists.

---

117 Dinges, Norman G., Yazzie, Myra L., and
Tollefson, Gwen D. *Developmental Intervention for
Navajo Family Mental Health*. Personnel Guidance
Journal 52(6):390-395, 1974.

This paper reports on a current program of assistance to
Navajo families. Within a developmental task framework,
family interaction activities were devised with due regard
for cultural considerations. Family programs were individualized. Other study designs are envisioned which may
further broaden the transcultural approach.

---

118 Doyle, Averil M., and Dorlac, Charles. *Treating Chronic Crisis Bearers and Their Families*.
Journal of Marriage and Family Counseling 4(3):
37-42, 1978.

The authors present a method for family crisis intervention, utilizing a case history approach. The goal is extended from restoring the crisis-bearing unit to its precrisis level of coping to a basic restructuring of maladaptive precrisis behaviors. This method is aimed at general
behavior change as well as resolution of the immediate
situation and adapts crisis intervention theory to intervention involving chronic crisis bearers and their families.

---

119 Dulfano, Celia. *Family Therapy of Alcoholism*.
In: Practical Approaches to Alcoholism Psychotherapy. New York: Plenum Press, 1978.

Psychotherapy of family units in which one or more members are alcoholic is described and illustrated with two case histories. It is felt that alcoholism is very much a family disease.

---

120 Dulicai, Dianne. *Nonverbal Assessment of Family Systems: A Preliminary Study.* Art of Psychotherapy 4(2):55-62, 1977.

The hypothesis of this preliminary study is that family interaction patterns and their affective qualities and messages are manifested in nonverbal behavior. Family interaction conflict and other pathology can therefore be detected through assessment of the nonverbal behavior and its deviations.

---

121 Epstein, Norman. *Techniques of Brief Therapy with Children and Parents.* Social Casework 57(5): 317-323, 1976.

The process and goals of parent-child therapy are described. Focused on present problems, the aim is to maximize parenting abilities in adults and growth-producing behaviors in children.

---

122 Fellner, Carl. *The Use of Teaching Stories in Conjoint Family Therapy.* Family Process 15(4): 427-431, 1976.

In this paper, a form of therapeutic communication called the teaching story is presented which embodies a mixture of both the educational and the paradoxical or the absurd.

---

123 Fengler, Joerg. *Feedback Technique in Marriage and Family Therapy.* Praxis der Psychotherapie 20(1):34-48, 1975.

The author relates how feedback works most effectively in interpersonal relationships. The therapist acts as observer, model, and counselor, and instructs the couple

or group in "rituals," which are verbal or nonverbal
exercises.

---

124 Fenyes, Cecile. *The Family Pride Factor in
Family Therapy. Family Therapy 3(2):129-132,
1976.*

One characteristic of families seeking help is the presence
of indicators of there being a low level of family pride.
Several interventions are described.

---

125 Fenyes, Cecile. *Kiss the Frog: A Therapeutic
Intervention for Reframing Family Rules. Family
Therapy 3(2):123-128, 1976.*

The author describes the intervention technique of
reframing, which applies to family situations involving
rigidified, polarized trait allocations among family members. The goal of this intervention is to enhance family
members' freedom to behave and to be perceived in positive terms along dimensions where they were formerly
perceived negatively in a stereotyped manner.

---

126 Figley, Charles R., and Sprenkle, Douglas H.
*Delayed Stress Response Syndrome: Family Therapy
Indications. Journal of Marriage and Family
Counseling 4(3):53-60, 1978.*

The theoretical nature of the delayed stress response
syndrome and its most characteristic symptoms are delineated within the context of treating Vietnam combat veter-
ans. This paper outlines treatment implications with a
family therapy program.

---

127 Filstead, William J. *Family, Alcohol Misuse,
and Alcoholism: Priorities and Proposals for
Intervention. Journal of Studies on Alcohol
38(7):1447-1454, 1977.*

Description of a conference, the main theme of which was
family intervention--i.e., treating the family, rather than

50

the individual, as the unit of concern. The overall senti-
ment of the participants was that a more generic approach
to alcohol problems might prove effective in bringing families to treatment at the earliest possible time.

---

128 Fisch, Marcia.   Homeostasis: A Key Concept in
Working with Alcoholic Families.   Family Therapy
3(2):133-139, 1976.

The idea of homeostasis is a key concept in therapy with
families having an alcoholic member.   Two case histories
emphasize a systems approach to treatment and illustrate
ways in which such families seek to maintain homeostasis.

---

129 Flanzer, Jerry P.   Family-Focused Management:
Treatment of Choice for Deviant and Dependent Families.   American Journal of Family Therapy 6(2):
25-31, 1978.

A family-focused approach based on a Maslovian hierar-
chial family-needs scale as the treatment of choice for
helping the dependent and/or deviant family cope and
improve their problemsolving abilities.

---

130 Flanzer, Jerry P.   Family Management in the
Treatment of Alcoholism.   British Journal of Alcohol and Alcoholism 13:45, 1978.

Two case histories illustrate a family-focused approach to
treating alcoholics, based on a five-part hierarchy of
basic needs, ranging from physical safety and food and
shelter, to socioeconomic environment, social interaction,
and family actualization.

---

131 Flanzer, Jerry P., and O'Brien, Gregory M.
Family Focused Treatment and Management: A Multi-
Discipline Training Approach.   In: Alcoholism and
Drug Dependence.   New York: Plenum Press, 1977.

The thought is expressed that the family approach to
alcoholism is an idea whose time has come, and that social

service agencies should take heed of this fact. The implications of this approach to family substitute systems such as halfway houses and group homes are discussed.

---

132 Fleischer, Gerald. Producing Effective Change in Impoverished, Disorganized Families: Is Family Therapy Enough? Family Therapy 2(3):277-289, 1975.

This article describes an impoverished, disorganized family whose treatment was handicapped because two significant family members were reluctant to attend therapy. Potential new roles for the family therapist are reviewed.

---

133 Foley, Vincent D. Alcoholism: A Family Systems Approach. Journal of Family Counseling 4:12-18, 1976.

This article examines the case of an alcoholic family and illustrates the major points of structural family therapy. It is suggested that the problem of the alcoholic family might be best viewed from a system point of view and best treated by interventions following structural theory.

---

134 Foley, Vincent D. Family Therapy with Black, Disadvantaged Families: Some Observations on Roles, Communication, and Technique. Journal of Marriage and Family Counseling 1(1):29-38, 1975.

A systems concept was used to evaluate role delineation and communicational patterns of black, disadvantaged families. In the light of the observations made, some suggestions regarding technique are offered, notably the use of multiple-family therapy as a way of increasing therapeutic effectiveness and facilitating movement in the system.

---

135 *Foley, Vincent D. Structural Family Therapy: One Approach to the Treatment of the Alcoholic Family. In: Family Treatment Methods in Alcohol Abuse and Alcoholism. Pittsburgh, Pennsylvania: University of Pittsburgh, 1976.*

The author concentrates on the structural therapy model in treating families for alcoholism, which involves the belief that all organisms have underlying structures or patterns which explain their behavior. The structural approach to family therapy views the family as a social organism with interdependent, related parts in which structure encompasses the behavior of the interrelated parts. Structuralism applied to a family system indicates that the interchanges taking place between members are constant and express the family as a unit.

---

136 *Fong, J.Y., Schneider, M., and Walls-Cooke, P. Multiple Family Group Therapy with a Tri-Therapist Team. Nursing Clinics of North America 13(4):685-699, 1978.*

In this paper, the authors describe their attempts to minimize personal and professional factors that may hinder a group or be deleterious to tri-therapists' working relationships.

---

137 *Fraiberg, Selma. Psychoanalysis and Social Work: A Re-examination of the Issues. Smith College Studies in Social Work 48(2):87-106, 1978.*

The author describes how the child development project applies psychoanalytical principles in treating multiproblem family members. Psychoanalytic methods are also valuable in breaking the chain of family pathology, which often passes down from parents to children in multiproblem families. Child abuse represents a common example of this passed-on behavior. Difficulties in training social work students in psychoanalytic techniques are discussed.

---

138 Framo, James L. Family of Origin as a Therapeutic Resource for Adults in Marital and Family
Therapy: You Can and Should Go Home Again. Family Process 15(2):193-210, 1976.

The author presents a general method of involving adults
who are in marital and family therapy in sessions with
their family of origin, offering a clinical application of the
author's depth-theoretical orientation. This method is
based on the thesis that current marital and family difficulties are elaborations of relationship problems of the
spouses in their original families.

---

139 Freedman, T. G., and Finnegan, L. P. Triads and
the Drug-Dependent Mother. Social Work 21:402-
404, 1976

Triadic family systems and social work intervention are
explored for understanding the family orientation toward
drug dependency, based upon a structural or environmental approach. It is suggested that two therapeutic
concepts may be helpful in using the family therapy
modality in the treatment of drug-dependent women: the
triangularity of family relationships, and the individual
development process.

---

140 Freeman, David S. The Family as a System:
Fact or Fantasy. Comprehensive Psychiatry 17(6):
735-747, 1976.

The author discusses a number of myths about how families function, provides clinical examples of such myths,
and discusses treatment strategies and techniques for
overcoming them.

---

141 Freeman, David S. The Use of Time in Family
Therapy. Family Therapy 4(3):195-206, 1977.

The use of phased treatment in family therapy is discussed. In each stage of family work, there are the
warming-up, working-hard, and winding-down phases.
The phases take place in each session, but the sessions

are considered to be the most crucial in laying the groundwork for future therapeutic progress.

---

142 Friesen, V.I. On Shame and the Family. Family Therapy 6(7):39-58, 1979.

This article discusses shame, a basic and powerful emotion seldom dealt with in the literature on family therapy. In working with families, the therapist must be sensitive to the issues of shame in himself as well as others and be prepared to confront pain and humiliation in an open, empathic, and impartial manner with a multigenerational perspective that will promote healthy individuation and emotional growth.

---

143 Gaines, Thomas. A Technique for Reducing Parental Obsessions in Family Therapy. Family Therapy 5(1):91-94, 1978.

A treatment exercise is described which involves having parents write down their obsessive thoughts about their children. In so doing, the parents can more objectively evaluate such fears. A case study is presented to illustrate the technique.

---

144 Gartner, Richard B., Bass, Anthony, and Wolbert, Sharon. The Use of the One-Way Mirror in Restructuring Family Boundaries. Family Therapy 6(1):27-37, 1979.

The authors describe the treatment of a family in which a one-way mirror was used as a semipermeable boundary erected to distance an adolescent boy from his parents' marital conflict. The practical and theoretical implications of the use of the one-way mirror in family therapy are discussed.

---

145 Giarretto, H. Humanistic Treatment of Father-Daughter Incest. Journal for Humanistic Psychology 18(4):59-76, 1978.

Family treatment using the principles of "humanistic psychology" is described for cases involving father-daughter incest.

---

146 Gootnick, Andrew T.   The Use of the Mini-
Contract in Family Therapy.   Family Therapy 3(2):
169-173, 1976.

A mini-contract is useful in family therapy when the focus of treatment is shifted from the family to an individual member.   The application of this concept is presented in extensive detail.

---

147 Grodner, B.   Family Systems Approach to Child
Abuse--Etiology and Intervention.   Journal of
Clinical Child Psychology 6(1):32-35, 1977.

Following a review of traditional child abuse causes and intervention theories, an   interactional family systems approach and its therapeutic application are described.

---

148 Gross, Gregory.   The Family Angel: The Scapegoat's Counterpart.   Family Therapy 6(3):133-136,
1979.

The author describes a type of dysfunctional family structure in which the "badness" of one child is balanced by the "goodness" of another.   Although the bad child is identified as the symptom carrier, both children in this devil/angel pattern are seen as acting out parental needs. The therapeutic techniques used to confront such a family system are discussed.

---

149 Haley, J.   Leaving Home: The Therapy of Disturbed Young People.   New York: McGraw-Hill,
1980.

Presents a system of therapy for helping disturbed young people and their families at the transitional stage when children are leaving home.   Case histories and excerpts from actual family interviews are used to cover a variety

56

of family issues. Presents effective methods which are adaptable to the wide range of families, life-styles, and problems encountered in actual practice.

---

150 Harbin, H.T. *Episodic Dyscontrol and Family Dynamics.* American Journal of Psychiatry 135(10): 1113-1116, 1977.

The author describes characteristics of patients, primarily adolescents, who suffer from episodic violent behavior and their relations with their families. Family therapy is the preferred treatment approach; treatment should be active, should initially focus on ways of handling dyscontrol episodes, and should emphasize that the patient is responsible for his or her actions.

---

151 Harbin, H.T. *Families and Hospitals: Collusion or Cooperation?* American Journal of Psychiatry 135(2):1496-1499, 1978.

The author describes the therapeutic problems that can arise on a family-oriented psychiatric inpatient service. The stress emerging from the therapeutic demands on and changes in the internal structure of the family may cause the family to seek to reestablish its internal equilibrium by changing the hospital staff and structure. These transactions between the hospital and families, which are complex, are extremely important to recognize because they can undermine the therapeutic process.

---

152 Hare-Mustin, Rachel T. *Family Therapy and Sex Role Stereotypes.* Counseling Psychologist 8(1): 31-32, 1979.

Several issues in family therapy as they relate to the counseling of women are discussed. Strategies needed to provide change opportunities for women involved in family therapy include the use of a formal contract delineating group members' rights, redefinition and reallocation of family work tasks, development of equality in communication patterns among family members, a clear definition of generational boundaries, and reinforcement of womens'

privacy and ownership rights in the family. Recommendations for counselors involved in family therapy are
included.

---

153 Hare-Mustin, Rachel T. A Feminist Approach to
Family Therapy. Family Process 17(2):181-194,
1978.

Although family therapy recognizes the importance of the
social context as a determiner of behavior, family therapists have not examined the consequences of traditional
socialization practices that primarily disadvantage women.
The unquestioned reinforcement of stereotyped sex roles
take place in much of family therapy.

---

154 Hare-Mustin, Rachel T. Paradoxical Tasks in
Family Therapy: Who Can Resist. Psychotherapy:
Theory, Research, and Practice 13(2):128-130,
1976.

The author considers the use of paradoxical tasks (PT)
as a solution to the basic problem of change in family
therapy. Attempting to change a system of dysfunctional
family interaction patterns frequently activates the processes which resist change. Instead of requiring change
from clients, PT's require the clients to intentionally continue their present behaviors and even to exaggerate
them.

---

155 Hartmann, Kathleen, and Bush, Mary. Action-
Oriented Family Therapy. American Journal of
Nursing 75(7):1184-1187, 1975.

This article describes a six-session family therapy program
conducted in the home of a troubled, but intact, black
family of four female and two male children and a mother
and father.

---

156 Heard, David B. Keith: A Case Study of
Structural Family Therapy. Family Process 17(3):
339-356, 1978.

This is an edited case presentation of marital therapy of a couple whose child was originally presented as the problem. Two primary themes are emphasized throughout the case. The first is that therapy consists of stages involving critical transitional points that need to be appropriately timed. The second is the use of a task to bring about structural realignment within the family.

---

157 Hill, Rodman. *Family Therapy Workshop: When the Family and the Therapist are of Different Races. Journal of Contemporary Psychotherapy 9(1):45-46, 1977.*

Participants in a workshop on the effects of race on patient-therapist relationships viewed videotapes of family therapy interviews and suggested that: (1) white clients tend more readily to trust black clinicians and expect to be well-cared for than do black clients treated by white clinicians; and (2) there is a danger that black clinicians will over-identify with their black clients.

---

158 Hindman, Margaret. *Family Therapy in Alcoholism. Alcohol Health and Research World 1(1):2-9, 1976.*

A review of the literature on the use of family therapy in alcoholism treatment shows it to be based on the concepts of improving communication, building trust, re-establishing satisfactory sexual relationships, and realigning parental responsibilities. Multiple-couples group therapy is a suggested form of family treatment.

---

159 Hirsch, R., and Imhof, J.E. *A Family Therapy Approach to the Treatment of Drug Abuse and Addiction. Journal of Psychedelic Drugs 7:181-185, 1975.*

An argument for family therapy of drug abusers is advanced, based on the experiences of the North Shore University Hospital Drug Treatment and Education Center.

An overview of the literature on drug abusers and their families is presented.

---

160 Hogg, William F., and Northman, John E. The Resonating Parental Bind and Delinquency. Family Therapy 16(1):21-26, 1979.

The resonating parental bind is a triangular family structure in which open conflicts exist between the parents, and the child (commonly adolescent) sides with one parent against the other in order to get his/her way in a given situation. When the parents move apart (e.g., towards divorce), or when they move towards conciliation, the child may resort to antisocial acts in order to maintain the customary condition between the parents, even though this results in contradictory situations, frustration, and rage for the child.

---

161 House, A.E., and Stambaugh, E.E. Transfer of Therapeutic Effects from Institution to Home: Faith, Hope, and Behavior Modification. Family Process 18(2):87-93, 1979.

Effective transfer of therapeutic results from institutional to home settings is a demanding problem facing family therapists. The issues involved and one approach to their solution are examined through the case of a 10-year-old boy hospitalized for severe antisocial behavior. The therapeutic program was faded out and concurrently faded into the home.

---

162 Howard, D.P., and Howard, N.T. Treatment of the Significant Other. In: Practical Approaches to Alcoholism Psychotherapy. New York: Plenum Press, 1978.

The philosophy and counseling techniques of the Howard Institute Family Counseling Center in Columbia, Missouri, are described, along with the Center's methods for reaching alcoholics' family members or significant others via public education and community awareness. Two case histories which illustrate this family therapy process are presented.

---

163 Howe, Bruce J. *Family Therapy and the Treatment of Drug Abuse Problems. Family Therapy 1(1):89-98, 1974.*

Potential roles for the family therapist in drug abuse treatment are described. The question of who is actually having a problem in cases of youthful drug abuse is considered, and drug use is seen as a way to bleed-off anxiety in a family or social system.

---

164 Howe, Bruce J., Howe, Shannon R., and Peck, Bruce B. *Working From the Outside: Administrative Considerations in the Psychotherapy of a Family with Disrupted Boundaries. Family Therapy 5(2):193-204, 1978.*

A network psychotherapist who tries to work in alliance with the growth and autoreparative potential of patients and their systems must first assess the condition of the system and subsystem boundaries. If they are too loose, as in a case described in this paper, the family will not be able to extrude him or her, and termination will not be possible. The therapist must therefore correct that problem at the outset. This can be done by creative structuring of the context surrounding the content of the therapy sessions--that is, it can be corrected administratively.

---

165 Huberty, Catherine E., and Huberty, David J. *Treating the Parents of Adolescent Drug Abusers. St. Cloud, Minnesota: Central Minnesota Mental Health Center, Detoxification and Halfway House Services, 1976.*

Using concepts of family therapy, the authors outline the theory and treatment for the parents of the adolescent chemical abuser. The approach used here, a parents' survival group, using a therapist-couple and focusing on the marriage relationship, restored the priority of the

marital relationship, and helped the parents to deal more
effectively with their adolescents' problems.

---

166 *Huberty, Catherine E., and Huberty, David J.*
Treating the Parents of Adolescent Drug Abusers.
Contemporary Drug Problems 5(4):573-592, 1976.

A program is presented for rehabilitating the marriages of
parents of drug-abusing youth. In such families, the
stability of the family unit may have suffered due to pre-
occupation with the child's addiction, the use of the
addiction to cover up marital problems, and the seeking
of homeostasis even when such equilibrium is negative.
The family constellation is explored by a family attribute
analysis that defines family roles and values.

---

167 *Huberty, David J.   Treating the Adolescent*
Drug Abuser: A Family Affair.   Contemporary Drug
Problems 4:179-194, 1975.

The case is made for family therapy in treating the adolescent drug abuser.   Topics discussed are the adolescent's family, stability of the family unit, circular
causality, mutual problem areas, and emancipation and
communication.

---

168 *Ishizuka, Ykio.   Conjoint Therapy for Marital*
Problems.   Psychiatric Annals 9(6):310-317, 1979.

The author discusses conjoint therapy for marital problems, including indications and contraindications, prognosis in therapy, the therapist's role, and techniques
used.   For example, positive indications for conjoint
therapy include occasions when individual therapy is at
an impasse, one spouse is threatened by the therapy of
the other, and there is a history or likelihood of acting-
out.

---

169 *Jaffe, Marilyn.   Repatterning an Ineffective*
Mother-Daughter Attachment.   Perspectives in
Psychiatric Care 14(1):34-39, 1976.

Therapeutic intervention in family therapy is discussed in terms of bringing the problem into a family focus; i.e., perceiving the problem as system-based rather than as residing in a problem individual. The tasks of the family therapist are listed and described.

---

170 Janzen, Curtis. *Family Treatment for Alcoholism: A Review.* Social Work 23(2):135-141, 1978.

Based on a review of the literature, the author presents a systems approach to understanding the interaction between the alcoholic, his or her drinking problem, and the family as a whole. Alcoholism is frequently seen as either the cause or the consequence of the pattern of family life.

---

171 Jefferson, Carter. *Some Notes on the Use of Family Sculpture in Therapy.* Family Process 17(1):69-76, 1978.

Therapists learning to use family sculpture as a tool often find difficulty in exploiting the technique to its fullest. This article, designed to encourage therapists to take the risks involved in using a technique new to them, describes how the author and his cotherapists used sculpture in different ways in three cases.

---

172 Johnson, Jackie, Weeks, Gerald R., and Labate, L. *Forced Holding: A Technique for Treating Parentified Children.* Family Therapy 6(3):123-132, 1979.

Presents the forced-holding technique as a method of intervention for reestablishing intergenerational boundaries between parent(s) and children where the child feels he/she is in charge or in power within the family. The method serves the function of rechanneling authority and power back to the parent(s).

---

173 *Johnson, Thomas F. A Contextual Approach to Treatment of Juvenile Offenders. Offender Rehabilitation 3(2):171-179, 1978.*

The questions of what activates delinquent behavior and what functions delinquency serves are considered. Delinquency is defined as occurring when the family system becomes dysfunctional and may serve as an effort to restore family functioning. A method of involving families in treatment is suggested.

---

174 *Johnson, Thomas F. Family Therapy with Families Having Delinquent Offspring. Journal of Family Counseling 3(2):32-37, 1975.*

Therapy with families of delinquent children often provokes a number of defensive maneuvers to avoid family involvement in solving their problems. Many families view delinquent behavior as others view psychopathology. The problem for the therapist in either case is to help the family past that point to a place where they can begin to deal with one another and work together to resolve their problems. A therapeutic technique is suggested, and different forms of resistance are discussed.

---

175 *Johnson, Thomas F. Hooking the Involuntary Family into Treatment: Family Therapy in a Juvenile Court Setting. Family Therapy 11(1): 79-82, 1974.*

This paper discusses ways of overcoming obstacles to therapy created by being in a court setting as an involuntary client.

---

176 *Justice, Blair, and Justice, Rita. Group Therapy Intervention Strategies for Abusing Parents and Evaluation of Results. In: Child Abuse and Neglect, Issues on Innovation and Implementation; Proceedings of the 2nd National Conference on Child Abuse and Neglect, April 17-20, 1977.*

A new approach to evaluation, the Goal Attainment Scale, is described as part of treatment in a group therapy process for child-abusing parents.

---

177 Katkin, S. *Charting as a Multipurpose Treatment Intervention for Family Therapy.* *Family Process 17(4):465-486, 1978.*

This paper discusses the behavior modification technique of charting as a double-bind communication. Its efficacy can be explained by integrating the viewpoints of behaviorist and family therapy approaches espoused by Haley and Weakland et al.

---

178 Kaufman, Edward. *Application of the Basic Principles of Family Therapy to the Treatment of Drug and Alcohol Abusers. In: Family Therapy of Drug and Alcohol Abuse.* New York: Gardner Press, 1979.

The major approaches to family therapy are presented and applied to the treatment of substance abusers. These approaches are described as: psychodynamics, structural, communications, experiential, and behavioral.

---

179 Kaufman, Edward, and Kaufmann, Pauline. *Family Therapy of Drug and Alcohol Abuse.* New York: Gardner Press, 1979.

This book conveys certain fundamental assumptions, based on the premise that alcohol and drug addiction are behavioral problems and that treatment methods should aim at "unlearning" the conditioned behavioral patterns of the addict.

---

180 Kaufman, Edward, and Kaufmann, Pauline. *Multiple Family Therapy: A New Direction in the Treatment of Drug Abusers. American Journal of Drug and Alcohol Abuse 4(4):467-478, 1977.*

Multiple family therapy is described as an important
treatment augmentation for drug abusers in a variety of
settings. The total family is viewed as being the patient,
with the drug abuser as a symptom bearer. Common family dynamics are described, as well as the techniques necessary to create structural changes in families.

---

181 Kazamias, N.   Intervening Briefly in the Family System.   International Journal of Social
Psychiatry 25(2):104-109, 1979.

A brief therapeutic intervention in a family is presented
with the use of the Synallactic Collective Image Technique
(S.C.I.T.).   The technique proves to be a very useful
tool for therapeutic intervention along general system
theory lines.   The S.C.I.T. makes use of family painting
as a second catalyst (the first one being the therapist) of
transaction.   It has been observed that such a brief and
intense intervention could lead, with proper handling, to
the reactivation of self-leading processes, which generate
more functional transaction within the family system.

---

182 Keeney, Bradford P., and Cromwell, Ronald E.
Toward Systemic Diagnosis.   Family Therapy 4(3):
225-236, 1977.

An alternative diagnostic epistemology is presented, based
on general systems theory.   A review of diagnostic styles
used by various family therapists shows that therapists
can be divided into those who think in terms of the whole
family process and those who include intrapersonal and
interpersonal processes in the diagnosis.   Systemic diagnosis is a way of understanding a problematic situation
by evaluating various systemic levels and their interaction.

---

183 Kelly, Brian J., and Gill, John D.   Gestalt
Approaches to Conjoint Therapy.   TPGA Journal
6(1):27-35, 1978.

Marriage and family counseling is one alternative to individual counseling.   It is the preferred mode of treatment

for all individuals except the social isolate who has no marriage or family structure. The specific methods by which persons avoid healthy contacts (introjection, projection, confluence, retroflection, and deflection) are discussed, as are counseling methodologies based on Gestalt and family systems theory.

---

184 Kiersh, E. Helping Juveniles by Helping Their Families. Corrections Magazine 5(4):54-61, 1979.

This article explains the concept of family therapy, investigates programs using this approach in delinquency prevention, and illustrates its effects upon individual cases.

---

185 Klabsbrun, M., and Davis, D.I. Substance Abuse and Family Interaction. Family Process 16:149-173, 1977.

The authors present the proposition that substance abuse may be understood and effectively treated when the individual abuser is viewed in the context of the family. Theoretical assumptions implied by this viewpoint are discussed. A selective literature review examines the available evidence that is relevant to this proposal and suggests areas for further empirical investigation.

---

186 Koehne, Nancy S. The User of Self as a Family Therapist. Perspectives in Psychiatric Care 14(1):29-33, 1976.

The author explores the possibility of using the self as a family therapist. This refers to the therapist's being himself or herself while giving treatment. An exercise for using the self is presented and discussed.

---

187 Kraemer, Sebastian. Tavistock Family Therapy Conference: A Review. Bulletin of the British Psychological Society 30:408, December 1977.

This article reports on the workshop "Family Therapy: Developing Techniques," held in Cambridge, England, in June 1977 by the Tavistock Institute. Several approaches and procedures were demonstrated and discussed.

---

188 Kramer, Charles H.   Becoming a Family Therapist.   New York: Human Services Press, 1980.

This book offers a detailed analysis of the process of becoming a family therapist. The author also examines the relative usefulness of various significant therapeutic techniques.

---

189 Krona, David A.   Parents as Treatment Partners
in Residential Care.   Child Welfare 58(2):91-96,
1980.

Full benefits of the use of parents as treatment partners in a residential care program are predicated upon involving them fully in the many aspects of assessment, treatment, and discharge decisions being made for their children.

---

190 Kroth, Jerome A.   Child Sexual Abuse: Analysis of a Family Therapy Approach.   Springfield,
Illinois: Charles C Thomas, 1979.

The Child Sexual Abuse Treatment Program (CSATP) uses self-help groups plus individual, family-group, marital, and play therapies to work with intrafamilial childhood sexual abuse. This book gives an empirical analysis of the CSATP humanistic family therapy model. The model emphasizes that punitive treatment lowers an individual's self-concept and increases pathological behavior.

---

191 Labate, Luciano, and Labate, Bess L.   The
Paradoxes of Intimacy.   Family Therapy 6(3):175-
184, 1979.

The importance of intimacy in dyadic relationships makes this concept a critical and crucial one to review and to explore in its therapeutic and human implications. Three paradoxes, derived from a definition of intimacy as sharing of hurt and of fears of being hurt, are considered in this paper: we need to be separate in order to be close; we hurt and are hurt by those we love the most; and we need to comfort and be comforted by those we have hurt or who have hurt us. Circular and linear solutions and resolutions for these paradoxes are suggested.

192 Lantz, James E. *Cotherapy Approach in Family Therapy.* Social Work 23(2):156-158, 1978.

The author contends that the co-therapy approach provides certain opportunities for therapeutic interaction that are not available in any other form of therapy. Four case illustrations are presented to demonstrate some specific advantages and practical considerations for using co-therapy in family therapy.

193 Larsen, John A. *Dysfunction in the Evangelical Family: Treatment Considerations.* Family Coordinator 27(3):261-267, 1978.

Religious families are seen as presenting a unique challenge to the nonreligious therapist. Although they differ from their nonreligious counterparts in important ways, religious families have not received attention in clinical literature.

194 Larson, Lyle E., and Fraser, Jennifer D. *Family Meal-Time Interaction: Understanding the Family in Its Natural Setting.* Canadian Counselor 13(2):58-67, 1973.

The authors observed and recorded interactions between seven members of a normal Canadian family during their evening meal. The number of messages sent and received, and their durations, content, and themes, were analyzed for each subject. These procedures provided informative and accurate indicators of the family system and processes.

195 Larson, Charles C., and Gilbertson, David L.
Reducing Family Resistance to Therapy Through a
Child Management Approach. Social Casework
58(10):620-623, 1977.

A series of child management classes teaches parents to
modify child behavior and opens up family communication.
Where child management techniques fail, the more dysfunctional families are then more readily engaged in treatment.

---

196 Larson, Charles C., and Talley, Leonora K.
Family Resistance to Therapy: A Model for Ser-
vices and Therapists' Roles. Child Welfare 56(2):
121-126, 1977.

A first step in treating a dysfunctional family unit is the
reduction of the family's resistance to therapy. A range
of approaches available for this task is discussed.

---

197 Laundergan, J. Clark, and Williams, Terence.
Hazelden: Evaluation of a Residential Family Pro-
gram. Alcohol Health and Research World 3(4):13-
16, 1979.

Family members and rehabilitation patients in the Hazelden
family program are provided with the opportunity to
receive short-term residential family therapy if they elect
to do so. The program process is described, and client
cognitive changes effected by the program are examined.

---

198 Leader, Arthur L. Denied Dependency in Family
Therapy. Social Casework 57(1):637-643, 1976.

Pathological denial of dependency needs is a source of
internal and family conflict. Family therapy sessions help
members explore and accept their varying hidden needs,
with the therapist providing reassurance and acting as a
role model. The therapist's attitude toward his or her
own dependency needs is important.

---

199 Leader, Arthur L. Intergenerational Separation Anxiety in Family Therapy. Social Casework 59(3):138-144, 1978.

Family therapy is advocated for dealing with pathological separation anxiety and fear of abandonment. Family members tend to replicate their early experiences neurotically in marriage and parenthood, forming symbiotic or rejecting relationships with spouse and children. Family therapy enables intervention during actual abandoning behavior.

---

200 Learning for Health Program, Center for Counseling and Psychotherapy, Santa Monica, California. Hospital and Community Psychiatry 29(3): 169-174, 1978.

Family relationships, behavior patterns, and the manner of responding to stress are important causal factors in physical illness and in health. Using case examples from his own practice as well as a review of the literature, the author demonstrates ways that families help create and complicate physical illness. Elements of this family therapy program that the author feels contribute to its success include helping the family focus on the past in relation to present concerns, investigating ways the family reacts to the illness, asking the patient why he is ill, conducting classes in stress release, and helping the family change patterns of interaction.

---

201 Leff, J.P. Developments in Family Treatment of Schizophrenia. Psychiatry Quarterly 51(3):216-232, 1979.

For the treatment of families of schizophrenics, the following issues are discussed: Is there any evidence that families cause schizophrenia? Is it useful to consider the family as a system? What is the aim of family therapy? Does family therapy work for any kind of family? Does family therapy work for families of schizophrenics? The conclusion is reached that systems theory can be applied successfully to some families when the patient suffers from certain conditions.

71

202 Lesoff, Reevah. What To Say When. Clinical Social Work Journal 5(1), 1977.

This article describes specific interventions and illustrates dialogue to implement a systematic approach to family therapy. This approach involves the following five steps: (1) elicit concrete behavioral goals; (2) elicit information about how the client has tried to implement these goals in the past; (3) elicit his or her ideas about why the behavior is occurring; (4) interpret how these ideas prevent the clients from insisting that the child change his or her behavior; and (5) undermine these ideas through appropriate questioning.

---

203 Levitt, Julie Meranze. A Family Systems Approach to Treatment of Child Abuse. In: Child Abuse and Neglect, Issues on Innovation and Implementation; Proceedings of the 2nd National Conference of Child Abuse and Neglect, April 17-20, 1977.

This paper considers the application of a family systems model to child abuse. The emphasis is on patterns of abuse and on the external and internal forces acting on the family and contributing to its behavior. Abuse is considered as just one of the possible destructive patterns that might result from the particular family organization. How to change those patterns becomes the focus of treatment.

---

204 Mandelbaum, Arthur. Diagnosis in Family Treatment. Bulletin of the Menninger Clinic 40(5): 497-504, 1976.

The principles of family treatment are discussed in reference to diagnosis. The author states that the process of family therapy blends inseparably with the diagnosis, although the family may have already diagnosed one or more of its members as the patient. The intimate involvement of the family therapist in the family, the family's ambivalent attitudes toward the therapist, transference distortions, and countertransference reactions all contribute to difficulty in diagnosis.

---

205 Mandelbaum, Arthur. A Family Centered
Approach to Residential Treatment. Bulletin of
the Menninger Clinic 41(1):27-39, 1977.

The importance of involving the family of an identified
patient directly in his or her residential treatment is discussed. Omitting psychoanalytically oriented family therapy from the psychotherapy of individual adolescent and
young adult patients can result in premature termination,
treatment failure, staff-splitting, and other unfortunate
consequences. A successful case illustration is given. It
is suggested that individual treatment may be longer and
harder when it does not include such family involvement.

---

206 Marion, Robert D. Working with Parents of
Abused and Neglected Children: A Counseling
Approach for Professionals and Lay People. In:
Child Abuse and Neglect, Issues on Innovation and
Implementation; Proceedings of the 2nd National
Conference on Child Abuse and Neglect,
April 17-20, 1977.

The author contends that now that the pendulum is
swinging back against the idea of removing abused children from the home, the concept of parent counseling is
advanced as the preferred mode of treatment. Skills that
workers should have for successful family encounters are
described.

---

207 McAdoo, Harriette. Family Therapy in the
Black Community. American Journal of Orthopsychiatry 47(7):75-79, 1977.

Black, upwardly mobile families face all the stresses
experienced by other families dealing with developmental
crises and economic changes, but are subject to the additional strain of discrimination. Treatment strategies

designed for the unique situation of the black family are proposed.

---

208 McAdoo, Harriette. A Review of the Literature Related to Family Therapy in the Black Community. Journal of Contemporary Psychotherapy 9(1):15-19, 1977.

This article reviews how black families have been viewed in the literature; examines the special stresses faced by blacks at all financial levels, who are coping with racism and differing economic status in their attempts to maintain stability while moving up the economic and social ladders; explores theories of social mobility and the role that the extended family structure plays in black families; and explores the practical implications of therapeutic approaches for the practitioner.

---

209 McKamy, Ray L. Multiple Family Therapy on an Alcohol Treatment Unit. Family Therapy 3(3):197-209, 1976.

The author traces the development of a multi-family treatment program in an alcoholic hospital unit and describes the experiences encountered by the therapists. Principles of family therapy are discussed, and case reports illustrating successful therapeutic techniques in areas such as support, confrontation, interpretation, and improvement in family communication are presented.

---

210 McKinley, Cameron K., et al. The Upwardly Mobile Negro Family in Therapy. Diseases of the Nervous System 31(10):710-715, 1970.

In three middle-class negro families, that had been initially referred for multiple-impact family therapy, striking similarities in family structure and functioning were noted.

---

211 McNeill, John S., and McBride, Mary L. Group
Therapy with Abusive Parents. Social Casework
60(1):36-42, 1979.

A group therapy program for abusive parents, which
focuses primarily on the marital relationship and secon-
darily on child abuse, is described. Parenting skills were
taught through the group, and referrals are made to a
separate parent effectiveness training group.

---

212 Meeks, Donald E. Family Therapy. In:
Alcoholism, edited by Ralph E. Tarter and
Arthur A. Sugarman. Reading, Massachusetts:
Addison-Wesley, 1976.

General system theory is applied to family therapy, and
research into interpersonal transactions in families is
reviewed. The family is seen as a small social system
which can be used to facilitate recovery and to minimize
the risks of drinking relapse.

---

213 Meisel, Susan S. The Treatment of Sexual
Problems in Marital and Family Therapy. Clinical
Social Work Journal 5(3):200-209, 1977.

Notes that for many couples and therapists, rapid treatment approaches to sexual difficulties are inappropriate or
ineffectual, yet the current literature addresses itself to
either sex therapy per se or marital therapy, and rarely
deals with an integration of the two. This paper presents
guidelines for assessing the sexual difficulties in the context of the relationship and outlines techniques for
addressing the sexual difficulties directly while maintaining a more traditional marital therapy approach.

---

214 Michaels, K.W., and Green, R.H. A Child Welfare Agency Project: Therapy for Families of
Status Offenders. Child Welfare 58(3):216-220,
1979.

A pilot project that provides therapy for families of status-offender youths has proved effective in reducing placements and costs.

---

215 *Miller, William Hansford.   Systematic Parent Training: Procedures, Cases, and Issues. Champaign, Illinois: Research Press, 1975.*

Systematic parent training focuses on effective and efficient mental health care which requires minimal time involvement from the counselor. Based on a social learning model, it provides the counselor with a systematic method for assessing parent-child interactions; developing goals, intervention strategies, and maintenance procedures; and assessing parents' individual differences.

---

216 *Milosavljevic, Petar.   Family Psychotherapy Within Social Psychiatry.   Anali Zavoda za Mentalno Zdravlje 7(4):77-83, 1975.*

The author discusses the development of family therapy after the standard psychotherapeutic techniques had been shown to be ineffective in the treatment of family problems. The importance of psychosocial assessment of the family as a whole is emphasized. Psychosocial and educational support should be provided, as well as the therapeutic approach being used to solve conflicting family relationships.

---

217 *Morgan, S.A., and Macey, M.J.   Three Assessment Tools for Family Therapy.   Journal of Psychiatric Nursing 16(3):39-42, 1978.*

In this paper, the authors attempt to utilize existing knowledge of the family and family therapy in order to develop a universal tool for family analysis. The assessment tools represent a conceptualization of the three phases of family analysis. Use of these assessment tools should aid the therapist in organizing the overwhelming volume of information that is obtained in a short amount of interviewing time.

---

218 Moroney, Robert M. *The Family as a Social Service: Implications for Policy and Practice.* Child Welfare 57(4):211-220, 1978.

The concept of the family as being an important social service in itself suggests the need for policies based on the interaction between families and other social institutions providing services. This view has important implications, particularly in the case of handicapped persons.

---

219 Mueller, Peter S., and Orfanidis, Monica M. *A Method of Co-Therapy for Schizophrenic Families.* Family Process 15(2):179-191, 1976.

This article describes a model of treatment for families in which one child has been given the diagnosis of schizophrenia. Male and female therapists adopt structured roles that are used as a paradigm for exploring family patterns.

---

220 Muri, Roy. *The Family and the Problem of Internalization.* British Journal of Medical Psychology 48(3):267-272, 1975.

The author attempts to integrate concepts derived from family therapy with psychoanalytic concepts. In particular, the nature and process of internalization is scrutinized in the light of family-role functioning.

---

221 Noone, R.J., and Reddig, R.L. *Case Studies in the Family Treatment of Drug Abuse.* Family Process 15(3):325-332, 1976.

Case illustrations are presented to demonstrate that drug abuse and behavior can be understood more clearly in the light of family loyalties and unresolved family crises than from the perspective that drug abusers are social deviates. Drug abuse is viewed as symptomatic of the family's difficulty in getting past a particular stage in its developmental life cycle. The therapist's tasks in clarifying these difficulties and in facilitating changes are outlined.

---

222 Palazzoli, Mara S., et al. A Ritualized Pre-
scription in Family Therapy: Odd Days and Even
Days. Journal of Marriage and Family Counseling
7(3):3-9, 1978.

Describes a therapeutic tactic, called "ritualized prescription," that is specifically aimed at breaking up those behaviors through which each parent disqualifies and sabotages the initiatives and directions of the other parent in his or her relation with the children.

---

223 Papp, Peggy. The Greek Chorus and Other Tech-
niques of Paradoxical Therapy. Family Process
19(1):45-57, 1980.

This paper describes some of the interventions developed for treating the family of symptomatic children. The interventions are based upon a differential diagnosis of the family system and upon an evaluation of that system's resistance to change. They are classified as compliance-based or defiance-based, depending upon the family's degree of anxiety, motivation, and resistance. Paradoxical interventions, which are defiance-based, are used as a clinical tool in dealing with resistance and circumventing the power struggle between therapist and family.

---

224 Papp, Peggy. Family Therapy: Full Length
Case Studies. New York: Gardner, 1977.

Twelve family therapists each present a case, describing the way in which they treated a particular family over a period of time. The case descriptions include the ideas behind the major therapeutic interventions, unexpected developments, mistakes, doubts, second thoughts, and outcomes.

---

225 Parloff, Morris B. Discussion: The Narcis-
sism of Small Differences--and Some Big Ones.
International Journal of Group Psychotherapy
26(3):311-319, 1976.

Three issues in family therapy are examined--the kinds
of patients treated, treatment setting and techniques, and
goals (mediating and ultimate goals).

226 Parry, J.K., and Young, A.K. *The Family as a
System in Hospital-Based Social Work.* Health and
Social Work 3(2):54-70, 1978.

Caring for disabled family members at home can create
stress that may exacerbate existing dysfunctions in the
family. By changing the orientation of hospital-based
social work from "disabled family member as burden" to
"family unit as an ongoing system," the authors have
succeeded in helping dysfunctional, disunited families
become functional family systems.

227 Perez, Jesus G. *Child Therapy Conducted
Through Family Therapy.* Revista de Psicologia,
Universidad de Monterrey 4(1):15-21, 1975.

The author briefly traces the development of family therapy and discusses the importance of family dynamics for
child development. The need to consider psychological
problems of children in their ecological context is emphasized. Socioeconomic and cultural factors that may lead
to conflict in the parental couple and engender changes
in their roles regarding each other, their children, and
their family of origin are examined. Examples of applications of family therapy to specific problems of children
are presented.

228 Prater, Gwendolyn S. *Family Therapy with
Black Families: Social Workers' and Clients' Perception.* Dissertation Abstracts International
38(8-A):5056-5057f, 1978.

Based on interviews with social workers who have worked
with black clients, and with the black clients themselves,
this work outlines the unique qualities of black family
therapies.

229 Press, Leonard. *Treating the Family. Mary-land State Medical Journal 24(1):32-35, 1975.*

A conceptual model for working with families of alcoholic patients is outlined. Erik Erikson's "community of life cycles" idea is stressed and related to clinical practice. An approach to the initial contract proposed by the thera-pist when working with families is discussed. Emphasis is placed on the idea of the family as a human system for promoting 'psychological and emotional growth. Difficulties encountered in working with troubled families are reviewed.

---

230 Puryear, Douglas A. *Helping People in Crisis. San Francisco: Josey-Bass, 1979.*

Defines crisis help as restoring healthier family function-ing in from 1 to no more than 8 hours of worker time. The author, a psychiatrist/teacher, here offers his experience in teaching his own practices to a wide range of nonpsychiatrist practitioners.

---

231 Ranieri, Ralph F., and Pratt, Theodore C. *Sibling Therapy. Social Work 23(5)418-419, 1978.*

Many advantages accrue when the sibling subsystem is treated as an adjunct to family therapy. They include: the chance for the children to be alone in an environment designed to explore their relationships; the opportunity to improve interpersonal skills that may be transferred to peer relationships; the likelihood (because of feelings of security stemming from familiarity in a sibling relationship) of less defensiveness and, consequently, faster progress; and the opportunity to clarify and express positive feel-ings toward each other.

---

232 Ransom, J.W., Schlesinger, S., and Derdeyn, A.P. *A Stepfamily in Formation. American Journal of Orthopsychiatry 36-43, 1979.*

The increasing incidence of step-parenthood requires that mental health clinicians develop skills for helping members of two families form a viable new family unit. This paper conceptualizes stages in the development of the reconstituted family. Case material describes a scapegoated child as the focus of conflict in one family's progression through these stages.

---

233 Rathbone-McCaun, Eloise, and Pierce, Robert. *Intergenerational Treatment Approach: An Alternative Model of Working with Abusive/Neglectful and Delinquent Prone Families. Family Therapy 5(2): 121-141, 1978.*

An intergenerational family therapy approach is described for the treatment of abusive families at-risk for delinquency among the children. The growing incidence of child abuse and its effect upon the risk of juvenile delinquency is considered. It is contended that intergenerational family therapy, involving more than the two nuclear family generations, may be indicated when there is evidence of intergenerational transmission of family violence. A clinical example is presented in which a juvenile offender beaten by his father was seen with his grandparents.

---

234 Reilly, Dennis M. *Family Factors in the Etiology and Treatment of Youthful Drug Abuse. Family Therapy 2(2):149-171, 1975.*

The author discusses a rationale for the use of time-limited conjoint family therapy with drug abusers and their families. Steps in the treatment process and therapeutic interventions are considered. A tentative profile of drug-abusing family systems and suggestions for future research in this area are presented.

---

235 Rice, David G. *The Male Spouse in Marital and Family Therapy. Counseling Psychologist 7(4):64-66, 1978.*

Certain techniques are presented for facilitating male involvement in therapy, including modeling the confortable and direct expression of feelings, the defusing of power and dominance issues, and working with a co-therapist to model a flexible pattern of relating.

---

236 Richman, J. The Family Therapy of Attempted Suicide. Family Process 18(2):131-142, 1979.

Suicidal behavior is a multi-determined act based upon a variety of factors, among which family tensions and patterns of interaction predominate. Family therapy, nevertheless, is under-utilized for suicidal situations because too few practitioners possess the requisite skills in both suicidology and family treatment. This paper attempts to integrate the two fields, describes some assessment procedures, and presents an account of the method of family therapy utilized by the author with suicidal persons.

---

237 Richman, J. Symbiosis, Empathy, Suicidal Behavior, and the Family. Suicide and Life-Threatening Behavior 8(3):139-149, 1978.

This paper discusses the theoretical concept of symbiosis and its clinical applications in suicidal situations. Symbiosis is defined as both a developmental phase characterized by a lack of differentiation between self and others and a relationship which is contingent upon the family and social network. A disturbed symbiosis is a major component in a suicide attempt. In family therapy, a repetition of older symbiotic relationships is frequently observed.

---

238 Rodriguez, L.J., Morgan, D.A., and Rodriguez, A.M. Engagement of the Family in the Treatment of the Hispanic Alcoholic: Two Miami Programs. COSSMHO's National Hispanic Conference on Families, 1979.

Experiences of two Miami programs in the treatment of Hispanic alcoholics and the utilization of their families in treatment are reported.

---

239 Rolfe, David J. Pre-marriage Contracts: An Aid to Couples Living with Parents. Family Coordinator 26(3):281-285, 1977.

This article describes the use of a pre-marriage contract in working with teenage couples and their parents. The contract is an aid in focusing on the practical aspects of marriage preparation, allowing more direct subsequent focus on the feelings of family members.

---

240 Roman, Mel. Family Secrets: The Experience of Emotional Crisis. New York: Time Books, 1979.

A series of case histories is used to show how family "secrets"--hidden conflicts buried deep in past generations or in the present--can undermine and cripple the emotional development of family members. Family rather than individual therapy is seen as the most effective treatment for emotional suffering.

---

241 Rosenberg, Jerome. Counseling the Parent of the Chronic Delinquent. In: Therapeutic Needs of the Family: Problems, Descriptions, and Therapeutic Approaches. Springfield, Illinois: Charles C Thomas, 1974.

This volume examines the concept of chronic delinquency and procedures for assessing the role of the parent in a particular family situation. Three models of intervention are described: a support model in which the therapist helps the parents adjust to the particular problems presented by their child; a change intervention model in which the parents learn to alter significantly their relationship with the child; and a dual intervention model in which the parents learn basic skills to work more effectively with their child.

---

242 Rosenberg, J.B., and Lindblad, M.B. Behavior Therapy in a Family Context: Treating Elective Mutism. Family Process 17(1):77-82, 1978.

This paper discusses the necessity of using both behavioral and family approaches in combination, while working with electively mute children. The symptom and its significance within the family system are presented, along with a rationale for avoiding the pitfalls of individual approaches with such children.

---

243 Rosenberg, John B. Two Is Better Than One:
Use of Behavioral Techniques Within a Structural
Family Therapy Model. Journal of Marriage and
Family Counseling 4(1):31-39, 1978.

Behavioral and family therapeutic techniques can be combined within the family context. The approach discussed is most helpful during the beginning to intermediate stages of family therapy and serves to provide the therapist with the necessary leverage to allow for effective intervention and change. Three case histories are presented to illustrate the techniques discussed.

---

244 Ross, Patricia T. A Diagnostic Technique for
Assessment of Parent-Child and Family Interaction
Patterns: The Family Puppet Technique--For Therapy with Families with Young Children. Family
Therapy 4(2):129-142, 1977.

The origin and use of the family puppet technique for working with families with young children is discussed. A case example illustrates the use of the technique and its effects.

---

245 Ross, Patricia T. The Little Girl, The Family
Therapist, and the Fairy-Tale; A True Fable:
Based on an Intensive Family Therapy with a Low
Socioeconomic Level Family Where a Little Child
was Identified Patient. Family Therapy 4(2):143-
150, 1977.

A case of family therapy is recounted in the form of a fairy tale with a happy ending. The author feels that there are analogies between this story and that told by James Thurber in "The 13 Clocks."

---

246 Rozansky, Phyllis A. *Family Resource Center: A Family Intervention Approach.* In: *Child Abuse and Neglect, Issues on Innovation and Implementation; Proceedings of the 2nd Annual Conference on Child Abuse and Neglect, April 17-20, 1977.*

This paper explores the role of one small agency in preventing child abuse. The center's focus is the family unit, and the program represents a comprehensive but flexible system of direct and indirect interventions to reduce family stress and restructure parenting behavior.

---

247 Russell, Alex. *Limitations of Family Therapy. Clinical Social Work Journal, Summer, pp. 83-92, 1976.*

Therapeutic difficulties in marital and family therapy that result from an inability to resolve value discrepancies between therapist and family are discussed. Two case studies are presented that illustrate that when acting-out adolescents are involved, a guarded prognosis (made due to the lack of a motivation to change) is reinforced by the presence of chronic pathology, cultural differences, and the unwillingness or inability of the family or couple to engage in a valid therapeutic contract.

---

248 Sager, Clifford J. *Marriage Contracts and Couples Therapy: Hidden Forces in Intimate Relationships. New York: Brunner/Mazel, 1976.*

Sager's book focuses on the fact that individuals enter into the marriage with some awareness of what they have to offer and what they expect from their partner. Seager sees the achievement of a mutually acceptable marriage contract as the goal of marital therapy. Further, the process of assessment, negotiation, and change are learned as mechanisms that clients can make use of in their relationships.

---

249 Saunders, Daniel. Marital Violence: Dimensions of the Problem and Modes of Intervention. Journal of Marriage and Family Counseling, pp. 43-52, January, 1977.

Saunders discusses intervention techniques for working with violent couples. He refutes the acceptability of the catharsis theory in cases involving physical aggression between spouses; instead, he proposes interventions that improve positive problem-solving abilities.

---

250 Saxon, W. Behavioral Contracting: Theory and Design. Child Welfare 58(8):523-529, 1979.

An agreement binding a worker and a client, or members of a family, to change specific, measurable behaviors is an effective way to achieve mutual benefits.

---

251 Schacter, Robert S. Kinetic Psychotherapy in the Treatment of Families. Family Coordinator 27(3):283-288, 1978.

Kinetic psychotherapy consists of several young children's games that facilitate interaction and mobilize feelings. When used as a mode of family therapy, this process enables the therapist to catalyze and observe change in the family's patterns of communication, interaction, and level of functioning, while involving members in a relatively nonthreatening situation.

---

252 Scheulen, D. Strategies of Family Therapy in Probation Assistance--Necessity and Concept. Bewaehrungshilfe 26(3):216-230, 1979.

A family-oriented approach to probation assistance is advocated, and the concept of family therapy is explained.

---

253 Schlachet, B.C. Rapid Intervention with Families in Crisis in a Court Setting. In: Family Violence. Scarborough, Ontario, Canada: Butterworth, 1978.

The rapid intervention project of the New York City family court is described. This unit provides immediate psychological evaluation of all parties involved in a spouse abuse or child abuse case.

---

254 Scholevar, G. Pirooz. *A Family Therapist Looks at the Problem of Incest.* Bulletin of the American Academy of Psychiatry and the Law 3(1): 25-31, 1975.

The problem of incest is discussed from the viewpoint of dynamic family interactions. Investigation of such cases has seldom included evaluation of the whole family and the possibility of a disordered family system. In the several cases reported, it appears obvious that patterns of interaction within the family were important.

---

255 Schregardus, D.J. *Youth Diversion and the Myth of Parental Indifference.* Police Chief 41(12):48-51, 1974.

This article presents an effective family counseling program for youthful drug abusers in liaison with the police, who provide referrals and follow-up on families who default in fulfilling the counseling contract.

---

256 Shapiro, Rodney J. *A Family Therapy Approach to Alcoholism.* Journal of Marriage and Family Counseling 3(4):71-78, 1977.

Recent studies strongly suggest that family therapy is a promising method of treatment for alcoholism. In this paper, a comprehensive treatment approach is proposed. Specific strategies are described that can enhance treatment success by reducing resistances and maximizing changes in dysfunctional family interaction patterns.

---

257 Shulamith, L., et al. *Effects of Alcoholism on the Family System.* Health and Social Work 4(4):111-127, 1979.

Because the family is a system, the alcoholism of one member affects all the others, who develop defenses and symptoms parallel to those of the alcoholic. The authors describe the "survival roles" members adopt that allow the system to maintain its equilibium and explain how this balance shifts as the family recovers.

---

258 Silverman, D.C. *Sharing the Crisis of Rape: Counseling the Mates and Families of Victims.* American Journal of Orthopsychiatry 48(1):166-173, 1978.

The involvement of mates and family members in counseling interventions designed to help victims of rape in their post-traumatic reconstitutive efforts is critical. Suggestions are offered for assisting those close to the woman in their attempts to explore and articulate the feelings and concerns about the crisis.

---

259 Smilkstein, Gabriel. *The Family APGAR: A Proposal for Family Function Test and its Use by Physicians.* Journal of Family Practice 6(6):1231-1239, 1978.

Understanding family function is an important aspect of patient care, yet a practical approach to the evaluation of family function by the physician has not yet been devised. This paper introduces a brief questionnaire designed to test five areas of family function: adaptability, partnership, growth, affection, and resolve (APGAR).

---

260 Solomon, Neil. *Homeostasis and Family Myth: An Overview of the Literature.* Family Therapy 3(1): 75-86, 1976.

The author discusses the concepts of homeostasis and the family myth as they are used in the literature on family therapy. The implications of these concepts for treatment of families are examined in the light of comments in the literature.

---

261 Solow, Robert A., and Cooper, Beatrice M.
Therapeutic Mobilization of Families Around Drug-
Induced Adolescent Crises.   Adolescent Psychiatry
3:237-248, 1974.

A treatment approach is described in which a social worker
conducts intensive, child-centered interviews with the
parents while a psychiatrist consults with the adolescent.
Two case studies of adolescent girls who were secretly on
drugs are presented.

---

262 Sowder, B., and Glynn, T.J.   Family Therapy--A
Summary of Selected Literature.   Washington, D.C.:
U.S. Government Printing Office, 1979.

This review summarizes literature on family therapy, with
emphasis on its effectiveness with drug and alcohol abusers and criminal populations.

---

263 Stedman, James M.   Behavior Therapy Strategies
as Applied to Family Therapy.   Family Therapy
4(3):217-224, 1977.

A case analysis of the use of social learning principles and
procedures in therapeutic work with the total family.   The
behaviorally oriented family therapist uses a social learning
framework to analyze the family and to form a plan.

---

264 Steinfeld, George J.   Decentering and Family
Process: A Marriage of Cognitive Therapies.
Journal of Marriage and Family Counseling 4(3):
61-69, 1978.

Extends the concept of decentering, as formulated by
Piaget, to describe how the child comes to understand his
or her impersonal world to include family patterns.   Ways
in which decentering can be used with rational emotive
therapy and transactional analysis, both cognitively oriented therapies, are presented.

---

265 Steinglass, Peter. Family Therapy in Alcohol-ism. In: Treatment and Rehabilitation of the Chronic Alcoholic, edited by Kissin and Begleiter. New York: Plenum Press, 1977.

Family therapy is examined as a treatment modality, including explanations of key concepts, such as the family system, homeostasis, and dysfunctional communication patterns. The adaptation of family theory to alcoholism therapy is traced. The alcoholic marriage is explained as one in which members have an equal stake in the perpetuation of the alcoholic symptom, even though the symptom is limited to one member.

---

266 Steinglass, Peter. The Home Observation Assessment Method (HOAM): Real-Time Naturalistic Observation of Families in Their Homes. Family Process 18(3):337-354, 1979.

The Home Observation Assessment Method (HOAM) is a new method developed to carry out objective coding of family interaction over extended time periods in a home setting. It is a computer-compatible coding system that permits on-line data reduction of interactional variables emphasizing contextual and structural dimensions of family behavior as well as some of the contradictions involved.

---

267 Straussner, S.L.A., Weinstein, D.L., and Hernandez, R. Effects of Alcoholism on the Family System. Health and Social Work 4(4):111-127, 1979.

Because the family is a system, the alcoholism of one member affects all the others, who develop defenses and symptoms parallel to those of the alcoholic. In addition, each member of an alcoholic family unit adopts one or more "survival roles" that enable a balanced family system to be maintained. These roles, their key effects on family interaction, and the ways in which the balance shifts as the family recovers, are described.

---

268 *Stumphauzer, J. S. Elimination of Stealing by Self-Reinforcement of Alternative Behavior and Family Contracting. In: Progress in Behavior Therapy with Delinquents. Springfield, Illinois, Charles C Thomas, 1979.*

This case study describes the successful treatment by family counseling of a 12-year-old girl who had stolen small objects or money almost daily for a period of 5 years. Similar therapy is recommended for all juveniles who steal.

---

269 *Suchotliff, L. Crisis Induction and Parental Involvement: A Prerequisite of Successful Treatment in an Inpatient Setting. Adolescence 13(52): 697-702, 1978.*

The utilization of a stress-induction model in conjunction with parental consultation within an inpatient setting makes it easier to conceptualize the relationship between problems the child has in the program, how they are handled, and the way problems are dealt with at home. Involving the parents in dealing with programs (crises) allows one to see first-hand how the family interacts under conditions of stress and permits systematic interventions into this system.

---

270 *Szapocznik, Jose, Scopetta, Mercedes A., and King, Olga E. Theory and Practice in Matching Treating to the Special Characteristics and Problems of Cuban Immigrants. Journal of Community Psychology 6(2):112-122, 1978.*

The implications for treatment of Cuban immigrants' preference for lineality in interpersonal relationships, a present-time orientation, an activity orientation, and subjugation to natural and environmental conditions, are discussed. Acculturation problems facing Cuban immigrant families and their implications for treatment are also discussed. It is concluded that ecological structural family therapy is a treatment of choice for acculturation-related dysfunctions of Cuban immigrant families.

---

*271 Tiller, J.W. Brief Family Therapy for Child-
hood Tic Syndrome. Family Process 17(2):217-223,
1978.*

This paper reports on the success of exclusively using
brief, analytically oriented outpatient family therapy in
treating an 8-year-old girl presenting with a short history
of multiple tics. No medicines were used, and the
patient remained asymptomatic 9 months after ceasing family therapy.

---

*272 Tucker, Bernice Z., and Dyson, Ernest. The
Family and the School: Utilizing Human Resources
to Promote Learning. Family Process 15(1):125-
141, 1976.*

A program was established in which family members, public school professional staff, and a consultant from a family theray unit work together, using processes of family
therapy, to reverse maladaptive school behavior of children
and facilitate constructive interactions both between the
family and the school and among school personnel. Some
of the outcomes of the program are discussed.

---

*273 Umana, Roseann, Gross, Steven J., and Cherney,
Marcia. Crisis in the Family: Three Approaches.
New York: Gardner Press, 1980.*

The author systematically examine three approaches to
intervention with families in crisis: family crisis intervention, family therapy, and crisis intervention. Each
approach is described in general terms with a focus on
treatment, efficacy and goals, intervention strategies, and
characteristics of the ideal client. Psychoanalytic, behavioral, and systems approaches are examined, along with
systematic descriptions of the assumptions, treatment
goals, focus of intervention, role and type of intervention, role and type of client, and setting specific to each.

---

274 Umbarger, Carter, and White, Stephen L. Rede-
fining the Problem: Individual Symptom and Family
System. American Journal of Family Therapy 6(2):
19-24, 1978.

When a family therapist encounters a family in trouble,
one of his or her first tasks is to "redefine" individual
symptoms into statements about the entire family system.
A case study illustrating this principle is presented. The
meaning of this redefinition, why it is important, and the
difficulties therapists and families have in accepting the
redefinition are discussed.

---

275 University of California, Davis, Center on
Administration of Criminal Justice. Family Coun-
seling and Diversion; Planning and Implementing
Programs for Juveniles: Final Report. Rockville,
Maryland, NCJRS Microfiche Program.

Conferences are described that are held to explain to
juvenile court judges, probation administrators, and
others, the family counseling approach to juvenile delinquency prevention. The conferences are sponsored by a
Sacramento diversion project.

---

276 Valentine, D. The Developmental Approach to
the Study of the Family: Implications for Prac-
tice. Child Welfare 59(6):347-355, 1980.

A framework for an approach to social work with families
that stresses the developmental tasks of the members and
the family as a whole.

---

277 Balmer, J., Voorhees, J.C., and Schapiro, E.
High-Impact Family Treatment--A Progress Report.
Juvenile and Family Court Journal 30(1):3-7, 1979.

High-impact family treatment (HIFT), a form of therapy
involving multiple therapists over a 2-day period for families of juvenile delinquents, is examined as a way of
reducing recidivism, especially among status offenders.

---

*278 Visher, Emily B., and Visher, John S.   Step-
families: A Guide to Working with Stepparents and
Stepchildren.   New York: Brunner/Mazel, 1979.*

This book gives an overview of the stepfamily, analyzes
the structure of the stepparent family, and reviews
research findings.   This is followed by an examination of
the individual adults, the marital couple, the children, and
the new family unit.   Separate chapters give clinical
approaches, specific treatment techniques, and practical
advice for the family unit and its components.

---

*279 Walker, Yvonne.   A Treatment Approach to Child
Abuse and Delinquency.   In: Child Abuse and
Neglect, Issues on Innovation and Implementation,
Proceedings of the 2nd Regional Conference on
Child Abuse and Neglect, April 17-20, 1977.*

This article describes a series of steps for assessing each
person in the family of the abused child, in terms of his
or her status in light of Maslow's hierarchy of needs.
Treatment plans are also detailed.

---

*280 Waters, David B.   Family Therapy as a Defense.
Journal of the American Academy of Child Psychiatry 15(3):464-476, 1976.*

The author studied seven white families that evidenced
similar patterns in treatment.   These families presented
requesting family therapy, and had an identified patient
whose symptoms spoke of attempts at independence.   Four
distinct phases of therapy were noted, culminating in the
termination of the family therapy by family consensus and
in the continuation of treatment for the parents.   In each
case, family therapy was selected by the parents as a
defense against examining their own relationship.   The
notion of a family focus as a resistance to change is discussed.

---

281 Weaver, P.C. *Alderscage Youth Service Bureau--Family Counseling Approach to Delinquent Youth--Self-Assessment Report, January 1, 1976-December 31, 1976. Rockville, Maryland, NCJRS Microfiche Program, 1977.*

Review of a project applying family counseling and systems analysis approaches to working with delinquent and predelinquent youth, thus providing a viable alternative for youth who encounter the criminal justice system.

---

282 Wegscheider, D., and Wegscheider, S. *Family Illness: Chemical Dependency. Mattituck, New York: TFL Press, 1978.*

Chemical dependency, such as alcohol addiction in a family member, is discussed as a family illness. The dynamics of the family systems are examined to determine the pathology of the illness and the best treatment.

---

283 Wendorf, D.J. *Family Therapy--An Innovative Approach in the Rehabilitation of Adult Probationers. Federal Probation 42(1):40-44, 1978.*

An innovative family therapy approach to the rehabilitation of adult probationers is described that was instituted by the McLennan County Adult Probation Department in Waco, Texas.

---

284 White, Stephen L. *Providing Family-Centered Consultation to a Juvenile Court in Massachusetts. Hospital and Community Psychiatry 27(10):692-693, 1976.*

A program of the Cambridge (Massachusetts) court clinic is described which provides family-centered consultation to the district juvenile court. Specifically, the clinic works with the families of youthful offenders through probation officers and judges as a means of preparing a family for a clinic referral, and to reduce the probability of an adjustment problem in the offender's siblings. This

95

approach resulted in a marked increase of referrals to the court clinic for family evaluations and therapy.

285 Wilner, Stefanie R., and Rau, John H. Family Systems Drawings. Family Therapy 3(3):245-267, 1976.

Paper illustrating the use of family systems drawings to convey the concept of the family as a system. Through this method, the concepts of scapegoating, symbiosis, schism, homeostasis, and the double bind are presented. Suggestions for alternative uses of this technique are also described.

286 Winder, Alvin E., Greif, Ann C., and Kelso, Evelyn P. Family Therapy: The Single Parent Family and the Battered Child. Family Therapy 3(2): 97-107, 1976.

The use of the concept of parentification in therapy with a single-parent family, one of whose members is a battered child, is discussed. An extensive case history and reference to the literature illustrates the treatment of this type of family.

287 Wolkenstein, Alan S. The Fear of Committing Child Abuse: A Discussion of Eight Families. Child Welfare 56(4):249-258, 1977.

Parents' neurotic fear of abusing their children--although no abuse has actually occurred--can respond to therapy if specific techniques such as family diagnostic evaluations are employed to resolve this special problem.

288 Zimberg, S. Psychotherapy with Alcoholics. In: Specialized Techniques in Individual Psychotherapy. New York: Brunner/Mazel, 1980.

An approach to the psychotherapy of alcoholics is presented in terms of varying levels of ability to control the impulse to drink. This goal-directed approach structures

an often amorphous treatment process. Complex therapeutic involvement of the family in treatment can be considered in relation to these fairly predictable stages in
the recovery process.

Research Studies

A large amount of research has been reported in the literature on family counseling. The studies annotated in this section range from bibliographic research, through clinical and quasi-experimental studies, to large-scale evaluative research on the outcomes of family counseling.

---

289 Aldoory, Shirley. *Research into Family Factors in Alcoholism.* Alcohol Health and Research World 3(4):2-6, 1979.

This article examines recent research in the psychosocial factors involved in alcoholism, and stresses the benefits of family treatment for this disease.

---

290 Alexander, James F., et al. *Systems-Behavioral Intervention with Families of Delinquents: Therapist Characteristics, Family Behavior, and Outcome.* Journal of Consulting and Clinical Psychology 44(4):656-664, 1976.

A clinical setting was used to evaluate therapist characteristics, therapist process, and family process in a short-term, systems-behavioral model of family intervention. Twenty-one families were designated by one of four degrees of therapy outcome. These designations were supported by nonreactive recidivism data and independently derived process data in which improved families showed greater supportive communications. A priory assessment of the 21 therapists' structuring and relationship skills were strong descriptors of outcome variance. Data suggest that therapist relationship skills, heretofore overlooked in the behavior modification literature, may be crucial determinants of therapy success.

---

291 Arnold, J.E., Levine, A.G., and Patterson, G.R. *Changes in Sibling Behavior Following Family Intervention.* In: Behavior Theory and Practice-- Annual Review, 1976. New York: Brunner/Mazel, 1976.

Changes in behavior of siblings of 27 boys judged predelinquent and referred for family behavior therapy intervention are documented.

292 Ausloos, G. *Adolescence, Delinquency, and
Family--Experiences from Family Therapy.* Annales
de Vaucresson 14:79-89, 1976-1977.

Cases of Swiss juvenile delinquents and their families who
received therapeutic treatment are described.

293 Baither, Richard C. *Family Therapy with
Adolescent Drug Abusers: A Review.* Journal of
Drug Education 8(4):337-343, 1978.

A brief review of the literature, including treatment
approaches, processes, goals, and programs, is presented.
Reasons for treating the family of the adolescent drug
abuser are discussed.

294 Baron, R. and Feeney, F. *Juvenile Diversion
Through Family Counseling--An Exemplary Project.*
Washington, D.C., U.S. Government Printing Office,
1976.

The development, operations, and results of the Sacramento County diversion project for juveniles are described,
and guidelines for the implementation of similar programs
in other communities are offered.

295 Beal, Don, and Duckro, Paul. *Family Counsel-
ing as an Alternative to Legal Action for the
Juvenile Status Offender.* Journal of Marriage and
Family Counseling, pp. 77-81, January, 1977.

Description and evaluation of the effectiveness of a family
counseling intervention program operating in a large south-
western city to deal with juvenile-status offenders.

296 Bird, H.W., and Schuham, A.I. Meeting Families' Treatment Needs Through a Family Psychotherapy Center. *Hospital and Center Psychiatry* 29(3):175-178, 1978.

Families receive a comprehensive, five-phase evaluation, at the end of which a panel of evaluators recommends the type of family therapy and the therapist most suited to deal with the central problem. During the center's first 2 years of operation, 42 families received a complete evaluation, 36 began treatment, 16 were rated as improved, and 5 were rated as unchanged.

---

297 Bogert, A.J., and French, A.P. *Successful Short-Term Family Therapy with Incarcerated Adolescents. Journal of Juvenile and Family Courts* 29(1):3-8, 1978.

First-offender youths were successfully rehabilitated through a treatment method that used short-term, family-type therapy in counseling the juveniles.

---

298 Boudouris, James. *Homicide and the Family. Journal of Marriage and Family*, pp. 667-676, November, 1971.

This is a report on the analysis of 6,389 homicides in Detroit during 1962-1968. The author discusses those classified as "Family Relations": this group comprises the largest homicide category. Boudouris looks at age-race-sex variables and proposes alternative intervention strategies for family counseling and crisis intervention.

---

299 Burdsal, C., and Buel, C.L. *A Short Term Community Based Early Stage Intervention Program for Behavior Problem Youth. Journal of Clinical Psychology* 36(1):226-249, 1980.

Describes an early-stage intervention program for delinquent youths, a short-term (6-month) and long-term (2.7-year) follow-up evaluation. The program consists of working with children through camping, family therapy, and working with the child's school. The short-term follow-up clearly indicates an overall positive trend in support of the program. Further investigations to isolate and study the effects of camping, family therapy, and the schools are being planned.

---

300 Byles, J.A., and Maurice, A. Juvenile Services Project--An Experiment in Delinquency Control. Canadian Journal of Criminology 21(2):155-165, 1979.

A 2-year follow-up study of 305 juveniles in an intensive family therapy program showed that the treatment group had a higher recidivism rate than controls, suggesting that counseling may not be a viable treatment method.

---

301 Christensen, Andrew, et al. Cost Effectiveness in Behavioral Family Therapy. Behavior Therapy 11(2):208-226, 1980.

Thirty-six families with problem children between the ages of 4 and 12 were randomly assigned to individual treatment, group treatment, or minimal contact bibliotherapy. All conditions received similar information about the behavioral management of children; only the format for therapy and the amount of therapist contact were different. Analysis of the data indicated the superiority of group and individual treatment conditions over the minimal contact, bibliotherapy condition. Although it required less than half the amount of professional time, the group condition performed as well as the individual therapy condition.

---

302 Coe, William C., and Black, David R. An Exploratory Study Evaluating a Behavioral Approach to Disrupted Family Interactions. Corrective and Social Psychiatry and Journal of Behavior Technology, Methods, and Therapy 22(4):46-49, 1976.

This article explores the feasibility of a large-scale study evaluating family operant therapy by comparing it with the usual mental health-clinic approach to children's behavioral

problems.   The outcome indicates that further study of
family operant therapy is warranted.

---

303 Coleman, Sandra B., and Davis, Donald I.   Family Therapy and Drug Abuse: A National Survey.
Family Process 17(1):21-29, 1979.

This report describes the results of a national study of
the role of family therapy in the drug abuse field.   Characteristics of agencies that work with families are
described, as well as the demographic characteristics and
psychological problems of the clients most apt to be
treated in family therapy.   The study also looks at the
role and structure of family therapy in the ecological system of the treatment institutions.   A profile of the family
therapists who are responsible for providing services to
families is presented.

---

304 Coleman, Sandra B., and Kaplan, Doreene J.   A
Profile of Family Therapists in the Drug-Abuse
Field.   American Journal of Drug and Alcohol Abuse
5(2):171-178, 1978.

A profile of 1,117 family therapists who were providing
treatment to families of recovering drug abusers is presented.   The data were derived from a national survey of
the current status of family therapy in the drug abuse
field.   Results provide extensive information on the education, training, personal background, caseload characteristics, and theoretical orientations of these therapists.

---

305 Coleman, Sandra B., and Stanton, M. Duncan.
An Index for Measuring Agency Involvement in Family Therapy.   Family Process 17(4):479-483, 1978.

The development is described of the Progress Index for
Family Therapy Programs, a 23-item instrument designed
to measure the relative involvement in family therapy by
treatment programs.   Results suggest that the Index may
be useful in assessment of family involvement of differing
agencies treating different populations.

---

*306 Crowe, Michael J. Conjoint Marital Therapy:
A Controlled Outcome Study. Psychological Medicine 8(4):623-636, 1978.*

Forty-two couples with marital problems were randomly
allocated to conjoint therapy of a directive, an interpreta-
tive, or a supportive (control) type. A semantic differential based on self-concept and view of partner, and a
global rating, showed the directive significantly superior
to the control procedure on several measures.

---

*307 Dewitt, Kathryn N. The Effectiveness of Fam-
ily Therapy: A Review of Outcome Research.
Archives of General Psychiatry 35(5):549-561,
1978.*

Outcome research was reviewed on the conjoint treatment
of families that involved at least two generations from a
total of 31 studies. Results from the 23 studies without
comparison groups show that conjoint family therapy has
an impact that is similar, but not superior, to nonconjoint
methods. The eight studies with comparison groups provide some evidence that conjoint treatment is superior to
no treatment and to treatment with nonconjoint methods.
Studies that examine the effect of factors (i.e., patient,
therapist, and technique) affecting the outcome of conjoint
treatment show that variations in these factors do have an
impact on the results. It is suggested that identifying
the proper criteria of change is important.

---

*308 Dunsted, C., and Lindsay, J. Psychopathology
and Psychotherapy of the Families--Aspects of
Bonding Failure. In: Concerning Child Abuse.
Edinburgh, Scotland: Churchill-Livingstone, 1975.*

This paper, while dealing with the medical aspects of child
abuse, specifically addresses systems of treatment and
prevention of abuse in the context of the whole family.
The paper is based on 110 cases from England.

---

309 Edwards, Griffith, Orford, Jim, and Egert, Stella. *Alcoholism: A Controlled Trial of "Treatment" and "Advice." Journal of Studies on Alcohol* 38(5):1004-1031, 1977.

The findings of a controlled-trial experiment bring expensive, long-term treatment regimens into question. One hundred married men were randomly assigned to a regular "treatment" or a single-session "advice" group. There were no significant differences between the two groups in sociodemographic characteristics or treatment history.

---

310 Fabri, J. *Youth Service Center--Second Chance for the Youthful Offender. Crime Prevention Review* 3(1):8-18, 1975.

Description and evaluation of a Fremont, California, juvenile referral project designed to produce a measurable impact on the degree of juvenile delinquency and crimes committed by delinquents. The center's major counseling mode is family counseling.

---

311 Fairfax County Office of Research and Statistics. *Fairfax County--Evaluation of the Family Systems Program Through December 1976.* Washington, D.C.: Government Printing Office, 1977.

Selected offense histories of a sample of cases participating in the family systems program in Fairfax, Virignia, were used to evaluate the program's effectiveness.

---

312 Finaly, Donald G. *Alcoholism: Illness or Problem in Interaction. Social Work* 19(4):398-405, 1974.

The concept is advanced that excessive drinking may be a symptom of a person's faulty interaction with his or her family and significant others. Studies using this social systems approach (e.g., in which the family is regarded as the basic unit for treatment) are evaluated.

---

313 Fisher, Barbara L., and Sprenkle, Douglas H. Therapists' Perceptions of Healthy Family Functioning. American Journal of Family Therapy 6(2): 9-18, 1978.

In an effort to define "healthy family functioning," theoretical concepts discussed in the literature were identified, categorized, and integrated into a list of 34 aspects. A healthy family is one in which members feel valued, supported, and safe. They can express themselves openly without fear of judgment, knowing that their opinions will be attended to carefully and empathically. Family members are able to negotiate and change when necessary.

---

314 Gaines, Thomas, and Stedman, James M. Influence of Separate Interviews on Clinicians' Evaluative Perceptions in Family Therapy. Journal of Consulting and Clinical Psychology 47(6):1138-1139, 1979.

Parents and identified patients of 68 families in both conjoint and separate assessment interviews were rated by 48 clinical staff and students according to the semantic differential technique. Each evaluating clinician saw the entire family in a conjoint interview and either the parents or the child identified as the patient during a separate interview. As predicted, clinicians who had separately interviewed identified patients rated them more favorably than did clinicians who had instead conducted separate interviews of parents. Ratings of parents, however, were unaffected by the separate interview variable.

---

315 Giannotti, Thomas John. Changes in Self-Concept and Perception of Parental Behavior Among Learning Disabled Elementary School Children as a Result of Parent Effectiveness Training. Ph.D. Dissertation. Dissertation Abstracts International 39(7):4137A, 1979.

The effects of a Parent Effectiveness Training (PET) program in fostering positive change in parental attitudes, child self-concepts, and children's perceptions of parental behavior were investigated in a learning-disabled sample.

PET was found to be a viable program for effecting positive change in the self-concept of learning disabled children, for promoting positive growth in children's perceptions of their parents and parental attitudes toward their
children, and in effecting positive behavioral change on
several classroom behaviors.

---

316 Goldstein, M.J., et al. Drug and Family Therapy in the Aftercare of Acute Schizophrenics.
Archives of General Psychiatry 35(10):1169-1177,
1978.

After a brief inpatient hospitalization, 104 acute, young
schizophrenics, stratified by premorbid adjustment, were
randomly assigned to one of four aftercare conditions for
a 6-week controlled trial. Conditions involved one of two
dose levels of fluphenazine enanthate (1 ml or 0.25 ml)
and presence or absence of crisis-oriented family therapy.
Relapses during the 6-week period and at 6-month
follow-up were least in patients who received both high-
dose and family therapy (0%) and greatest (48%) in the
low-dose, no-therapy group.

---

317 Gurman, Alan S., and Kniskern, David P.
Behavioral Marriage Therapy: II. Empirical Perspective. Family Process 17(2):139-148, 1978.

Places research on behavioral couples therapy in the
broader context of outcome research on nonbehavioral
marital therapy. The authors conclude that an open mind
to all sources of data on the efficacy of marital therapy is
needed if meaningful advances are to be made in the
field.

---

318 Gurman, Alan S., and Kniskern, David P.
Deterioration in Marital and Family Therapy:
Empirical, Clinical, and Conceptual Issues. Fam-
ily Process 17(1):3-20, 1978.

Discusses recent empirical evidence of deterioration during
nonbehavioral and behavioral marital and family therapy,
based on the author's analysis of over 200 reports and

studies. Five case illustrations of deterioration in marital-family therapy are presented. While the frequency of patient worsening in marital-family therapy does not appear to exceed that previously found for individual psychotherapy, the acceptability of the evidence for negative effects in the treatment of systems may be greater than that which exists for individual treatment.

---

319 Harbin, H.T., and Maziar, H.M. The Families of Drug Abusers: A Literature Review. Family Process 14:411-431, 1975.

Reviews all relevant literature concerning the family background of compulsive drug abusers. The main content of the completed research (clinical studies, clinical studies with quantitative results, and controlled research studies) are summarized, and methodological criticisms are made. Future considerations for research on families of drug abusers are suggested.

---

320 Hedberg, Allan G., and Campbell, Lowell. A Comparison of Four Behavioral Treatments of Alcoholism. Journal of Behavior Therapy and Experimental Psychiatry 5(3-4):251-256, 1974.

Forty-five male and four female alcoholics were treated either with behavioral family counseling, systematic desensitization, cover sensitizations, or a shock presentation treatment program. Data indicate that behavioral family counseling was the most effective alcoholism treatment method of the four procedures studied.

---

321 Hirsch, Robert, and Imhof, John E. A Family Therapy Approach to the Treatment of Drug Abuse and Addiction. Journal of Psychedelic Drugs 7(2): 181-185, 1975.

This paper suggests ways of using the family dynamics of the addict as a tool for evaluating and working with addicts and their families. Observations are presented based on an evaluation of 47 families of drug addicts observed during the intake procedure of a hospital drug program.   Characteristic interactional dynamics are described, and the potential of a family therapy approach to drug abuse is emphasized.

---

322 Hung, John H., and Rosenthal, Ted.   Therapeutic Videotaped Playback: A Critical Review. Advances in Our Research and Therapy 1:103-135, 1978.

Research published on therapeutic videotape recorded playback (VTRP) applications is reviewed.   The use of playback in marital and family therapy, treatment of alcoholics, therapy with inpatients, improving social competencies, and other miscellaneous settings, are independently examined and evaluated.

---

323 Janzen, Curtis.   Families in the Treatment of Alcoholism.   Journal of Studies on Alcohol 38(1): 114-130, 1977.

This review of the literature on the family treatment of alcoholism suggests that, although there is no single definition of family therapy nor one single theory behind it, there is agreement that family therapy can be beneficial for both the alcoholic and the family.   While most of the family treatment reported was concurrent with or subsequent to other treatment, the success of family treatment for both the alcoholic and the family does not appear to be contingent on additional treatment.

---

324 Janzen, Curtis.   Family Treatment for Alcoholism: A Review.   Social Work 23(2):135-141, 1978.

This article reviews the social work literature in an attempt to clarify the nature of the relationship between the problems of the family and the problem of alcoholism. The author emphasizes that families of alcoholics are transacting systems.   The review concludes with an explanation of how family systems theory can be better applied to treatment of an alcoholic's family relationships. Examples of several treatment programs are presented.

---

325 Johnson, Theodore M., and Malony, H. Newton.
*Effects of Short-Term Family Therapy on Patterns
of Verbal Interchange in Disturbed Families.* Family Therapy 4(3):207-215, 1977.

Assessed the effectiveness of family therapy in changing
patterns of verbal interchange in disturbed families.
Twenty-eight families were treated with either family therapy or alternate treatment (family members counseled
individually). Family therapy was more effective in producing change toward egalitarian participation than was
the alternate treatment method.

---

326 Johnson, T.F. *Results of Family Therapy with
Juvenile Offenders.* Juvenile Justice 28(4):29-33,
1977.

Results are reported from an evaluation of family therapy
with juvenile offenders which assumes that the family system is the principal contributor to delinquency.

---

327 Kauffmann, Edward, ed. *Family Therapy of Drug
and Alcohol Abuse.* New York: John Wiley and
Sons, 1979.

This collection of articles gives clinical impressions and
population characteristics of drug and alcohol abusers and
their families. Family therapy techniques, especially the
systems approach, are described, and outcome data are
included.

---

328 Kinston, Warren, and Bentovim, Arnon. *Brief
Focal Family Therapy When the Child is the Referred Patient: II. Methodology and Results.* Journal of Child Psychology and Psychiatry and Allied
Disciplines 19(2):119-143, 1978.

The authors describe the experience of a workshop set up
within a department of child psychiatry to foster family
therapy and to develop a brief focal technique. Details
are provided of the first 29 cases. The pattern of child

and family improvement supported the theory that a symptomatic child can be a manifestation of family pathology.

---

329 *Klein, Nanci, Alexander, James F., and Parsons, Bruce V. Impact of Family Systems Intervention on Recidivism and Sibling Delinquency: A Model of Primary Prevention and Program Evaluation.* 'Journal of Consulting and Clinical Psychology 45(3):469-474, 1977.*

Eighty-six families of 38 male and 48 female 13-16 year-old delinquents were randomly assigned to one of four treatment conditions: no treatment controls, a client-centered family approach, an eclectic-dynamic approach, and a behaviorally oriented, short-term family systems approach. The family systems approach, when compared to the other conditions, produced significant improvements in process measures and a significant reduction in recidivism.

---

330 *Klopper, E.J., et al. A Multi-Method Investigation of Two Family Constructs.* Family Process 17(1):83-93, 1978.*

Two family constructs--prominence and interpersonal distance--are examined. The validity of each construct is investigated using data obtained from 15 families with a symptom-bearing child. Validity is supported in both cases through the occurrence of significant correlations among different measures of the same construct.

---

331 *Korth, J.A. Child Sexual Abuse--Analysis of a Family Therapy Approach. Springfield, Illinois:* Charles C Thomas, 1979.*

Originating as an evaluation study, but consequently developing into data base research, this empirical analysis focuses on family therapy as practiced by a child sexual abuse treatment program.

---

*332 Lask, B., and Matthew, D. Childhood Asthma.
A Controlled Trial of Family Psychotherapy.
Archives of Diseases of Children 54(2):116-119,
1979.*

In an attempt to evaluate the effectiveness of family psychotherapy as an adjunct to conventional treatment in
childhood asthma, children with moderate to sever asthma
were randomly allocated to a control group or to an experimental group; the latter group received 6 hours of family
treatment during a 4-month period. The experimental
group were significantly better in a day-wheeze score and
thoracic gas volume.

---

*333 Lewis, Alice Gates. The Impact of Parent
Effectiveness Training on Parent Attitudes and
Children's Behavior. Ed.D Dissertation. Dissertation Abstracts International 39(12):7245-A,
1979.*

The impact of standardized Parent Effectiveness Training
(PET) on parent attitudes and child behavior was examined in 60 randomly chosen parents. PET did not appear
to have measurable effect on parental attitudes as measured by the Parent Attitude Survey Scale or the Dogma-
tism Scale.

---

*334 Maskin, M.B. The Differential Impact of Work-
Oriented Communication-Oriented Juvenile Correction Programs Upon Recidivism Rates in Delinquent
Males. Journal of Clinical Psychology 32(2):432-
433, 1976.*

This study examines recidivism rates in work-oriented and
communication-oriented juvenile delinquency programs for
males. The results suggest that: facilitation of family
interaction and communication is related closely to successful treatment of the delinquent and consequent recidivism;
group counseling that provides the youth and parents with
an opportunity to learn better communication skills appears

to improve family cohesion and solidarity; and newer therapeutic approaches in delinquency should concentrate on filial and family-type therapies.

---

335 Masten, A. S. *Family Therapy as a Treatment for Children: A Critical Review of Outcome Research.* Family Process 18(3):323-335, 1979.

The value of family therapy as a treatment for child psychopathology is considered by reviewing pertinent outcome research. Some empirical evidence does exist that family therapy is an effective treatment for children--the data from studies of adolescents are especially encouraging. However, insufficient data are available for comparing the relative merits of conjoint family treatment and individual child therapy.

---

336 Master, Roshan S. *Family Therapy in Child and Adolescent Psychiatry: A Review of Families.* Child Psychiatry Quarterly 11(3):70-82, 1978.

A retrospective study of 35 families who received family therapy revealed that 40 percent dropped out after the first six-to-ten sessions despite precautions taken to accept only motivated families. The clinical impression is that family therapy with families having antisocial children proved to be a failure. The families who successfully completed the treatment communicated better, developed mutual understanding, and grew in tolerance for each other. Pathological hatred and rejection were replaced by acceptance and adequate amounts of love and family harmony.

---

337 Menne, J. *Iowa Research in Family Therapy with Families of Delinquent Youth--Final Report.* Eldora, Iowa: Iowa Training School for Boys, 1975.

This report explores what value family therapy has to offer for families of delinquent youth and who can benefit from it.

---

338 *Michaels, K.W., and Green, R.H. Child Welfare Agency Project--Therapy for Families of Status Offenders. Child Welfare 58(3):216-220, 1979.*

The work of children's services of York County, Pennsylvania, with status offender youths is examined. Therapeutic intervention with the family also appears effective in avoiding placement of the youth outside his own home. Tables and list of references are provided.

---

339 *Moos, R.H., and Moos, B.S. A Typology of Family Social Environments. Family Process 15(4): 357-371, 1976.*

A sample of 100 families measured on 10 dimensions of their social environments was subjected to cluster analysis to develop an empirically based taxonomy of families. Six distinctive clusters of families were identified: Expression-Oriented, Structure-Oriented, Independence-Oriented, Achievement-Oriented, Moral/Religious-Oriented, and Conflict-Oriented. An empirically derived taxonomy of the social environments of families may help to understand how different family environments are linked to different family outcomes.

---

340 *Nassau County Department of Drug and Alcohol Addiction. Alcoholism Treatment Services for Children of Alcoholics. Mineola, New York, 1979.*

Services delivered by the Nassau County Department of Drug and Alcohol Addiction to children of alcoholics through an outpatient alcoholism treatment unit are described. Problem areas identified as the children's program was developed include providing for an adequate length of treatment, family involvement, and separate groups for children and parents.

---

341 *National Institute on Drug Abuse. The Use of Family Therapy in Drug Abuse Treatment: A National Survey. Services Research Reports, 1977.*

This survey explores the nature and extent of use of family therapy practiced by drug abuse treatment and rehabilitation agencies. Recommendations are made for the increased use of family therapy and a comprehensive training program for family therapists in the addictions field.

---

342 O'Connor, D. *Domestic Violence Assistance Organizations--Summary Report. Washington, D.C.: ACTION, 1978.*

Results are given of a survey of 400 domestic violence organizations in the United States and Puerto Rico. The survey included an application for a regional project grant as an incentive for responding. Statistics on the prevalence of family counseling are included.

---

343 Orford, Jim, and Edwards, Griffith. *Alcoholism. Oxford, England: Oxford University Press, 1977.*

Factors within marriage that influence alcoholism treatment outcome were investigated in a sample of 100 families in which the man was an alcohol abuser. One factor significantly predictive of a good outcome for the husband in either group was marital cohesion.

---

344 Orford, Jim, Oppenheimer, Edna, and Edwards, Griffith. *Abstinence or Control: The Outcome for Excessive Drinkers Two Years After Consultation. Behavior Research and Therapy 14(6):409-418, 1976.*

Results are given of a 2-year follow-up of 65 married alcohol abusers who participated with their wives in an experimental family treatment program with comparisons of outcome at 12 and 24 months. An interaction between degree of dependence, type of treatment, and goal of treatment is noted. The implications of these findings for comprehensive alcoholism treatment services are given.

---

*345 Pinsof, W. M.   The Family Therapist Behavior
Scale (FTBS):   Development and Evaluation of a
Coding System.   Family Process 18(4):451-461,
1978.*

This study evaluated the validity and reliability of a new
coding system--the Family Therapist Behavior Scale
(FTBS)--that was designed to identify and study clinically
relevant verbal behaviors of short-term, problem-oriented
family therapists. Validity was assessed by testing the
scale's ability to discriminate significant, predicted differences between the in-therapy behaviors of eight beginning
family therapists conducting observed interviews and eight
advanced family therapists conducting supervisory interviews.

---

*346 Plummer, C. C., Merritt, K. A., and Leach, A. G.
Family Counselors and Law Enforcement--Hayward's
(CA) Approach to Domestic Violence.   Crime Preven-
tion Review 6(2):10-16, 1979.*

The Hayward, California, police department's experience
with using family counselors to assist in the handling of
domestic disputes is discussed.

---

*347 Rakoff, V. M., Sigal, J. J., and Epstein, N. B.
Predictions of Therapeutic Process in Conjoint
Family Therapy.   Archives of General Psychiatry
32(8):1013-1017, 1975.*

Following diagnostic interviews with 20 families in an outpatient psychiatric clinic, therapists made predictions of
the anticipated responses of the families to therapy. The
families' responses to the process of therapy was predicted
in a questionnaire. All predictions erred in the direction
of underrating the over-all effectiveness of conjoint family
therapy.

---

*348 Russell, C. S.   Circumplex Model of Marital and
Family Systems: III.   Empirical Evaluation with
Families.   Family Process 18(1):29-45, 1979.*

This study was designed to test the circumplex model of family systems that hypothesizes moderate family cohesion and moderate adaptability to be more functional than either extreme. Analysis of the study data yielded considerable support for the circumplex model. High family functioning was associated with moderate family cohesion on these dimensions. As predicted, high family support and creativity were also related to high family functioning.

---

349 Schofield, Rodney. *Parent Group Education and Student Self-Esteem. Social Work in Education 1(2):26-33, 1979.*

Rodney Schofield studied the effects of parent education on the self-esteem of third, fourth, fifth, and sixth graders. He compared PET with a behavior modification model, and found similar positive self-esteem gains just after the completion of both programs.

---

350 Sigal, John J., Barrs, Carol B., and Doubilet, Andrea L. *Problems in Measuring the Success of Family Therapy in a Common Clinical Setting: Impasse and Solutions. Family Process 15(2):225-223, 1976.*

Sixty-two families that were treated in conjoint therapy in the outpatient clinic of a general community hospital for about a year and 31 families that refused further contact with the same clinic after two or fewer interviews, were followed up 4½ years later. The main difference found in the two groups was that the treated group reported exhibiting more new symptoms. The complexities of interpreting the date obtained are used as a basis for discussing problems that confront, and may deter, clinics attempting to evaluate their clinical work by means of controlled, nonfactorial, or related designs.

---

351 Slipp, S., and Kressel, K. *Difficulties in Family Therapy Evaluation. I. A Comparison of Insight vs. Problem-Solving Approaches. II. Design Critique and Recommendations. Family Process 4(17):409-422, 1978.*

In Part I, an outcome study comparing two methods of family treatment is reported. In Part II, the study is critically reviewed. The practical obstacles to implementing an experimental design in a clinic setting are considered.

---

352 Sowder, B., Dickey, S. and Glynn, T.J. *Family Therapy: A Summary of Selected Literature. NIDA Service Research Monograph Series. Washington, D.C.: U.S. Government Printing Office, 1980.*

This work presents a review of selected literature written or published through 1977. Specifically, it provides an overview of the findings from empirical research designed to determine the effectiveness of family therapy with drug and alcohol abusers and criminal populations.

---

353 Stanley, Sheila. *Family Education to Enhance the Moral Atmosphere of the Family and the Moral Development of Adolescents. Journal of Counseling Psychology 25(2):110-118, 1978.*

The author studied the effects of a course for families about democratic conflict resolution on families' collective decision-making abilities and on the moral reasoning of adolescent participants. Sixteen couples and their adolescent children were divided into three groups: parents and their adolescents, parents only, and a control group. Both experimental groups received Parent Effectiveness Training, and received training in Adlerian approaches to conflict resolution and how to conduct family meetings. Parents in both experimental groups significantly increased their egalitarian attitudes toward family decisionmaking. Families in both experimental groups significantly improved their effectiveness in collective decisionmaking.

---

354 Stanton, M.D. *Family Treatment Approaches to Drug Abuse Problems: A Review. Family Process 18(3):251-280, 1979.*

This review covers the literature that has emerged specifically on the family treatment of drug abuse problems.

Following a brief discussion of patterns and structures prevalent in drug-abusing families, 68 different studies or programs (discussed in 74 papers) are compared as to their techniques and results. It is concluded that family treatment for drug abuse is gaining widespread acceptance and shows considerable promise for dealing effectively with problems of this type.

---

355 Stanton, M.D. *Family Treatment of Drug Problems. Washington, D.C.: U.S. Department of Health and Human Services, 1979.*

Various forms of family treatment approaches that have been applied to drug problems are reviewed, along with the significant results of such treatment.

---

356 Stedman, James M., Gaines, Thomas, and Morris, Robin. *A Study of Conceptualization of Family Structure by Experienced Family Therapists. Family Therapy 6(3):177-142, 1979.*

The authors examine how experienced family therapists conceptualized family structure on an initial assessment of 100 intact and single-parent families. The clinicians' conceptual structures were measured using the semantic differential technique, and data were analyzed by Wilcoxon signed-rank tests. Results show that SS linked the "whole family" concept with both mother and child.

---

357 Steinglass, Peter. *Experimenting with Family Treatment Approaches to Alcoholism, 1950-1975: A Review. Family Process 15(7):97-123, 1976.*

A critical review assessing 25 years of experimental and clinical literature is presented on family treatment approaches to alcoholism. The historical development on family therapy is described in four distinct stages which are reflected in the existing literature: initial interest in the "alcoholic family"; experimentation with concurrent group therapy techniques; application of new family theory concepts to alcoholism; and tentative use of more traditional family therapy techniques for alcoholism.

---

358 Steinglass, Peter. *Research: Alcohol as a Member of the Family. Human Ecology Forum 9(3): 9-11, 1978.*

The following topics are discussed: alcoholism in the family; parents and alcoholism; family systems and the chronic phase; family treatment approaches to alcoholism; and public policy toward alcoholism.

---

359 Steinglass, Peter, Davis, Donald I., and Berenson, David. *Observations of Conjointly Hospitalized "Alcoholic Couples" During Sobriety and Intoxication: Implications for Theory and Therapy. Family Process 16(2):1-16, 1977.*

Clinical data are presented from a research study designed to examine interactional behavior in alcoholic couples. An innovative feature of the study was the simultaneous admission of three couples to an inpatient setting in which at least one of the members was an alcoholic. The inpatient experience was part of an intensive, 6-week, multiple-couples, group therapy program.

---

360 Straker, G., and Jacobson, R. *A Study of the Relationship Between Family Interaction and Individual Symptomology Over Time. Family Process 18(4):443-450, 1979.*

This study was designed to answer two questions: Can a relationship over time between family interaction and individual symptomatology be demonstrated? Can it be shown that changes in interaction have more influence on changes in the symptom than vice versa? The results of the analyses answered both questions in the affirmative, thus supporting the rationale underlying family therapy.

---

361 Stratton, J.G. Effects of Crisis Intervention
Counseling on Predelinquent Misdemeanor Juvenile
Offenders. Juvenile Justice 26(4):7-18, 1975.

This is a report on a study which investigated whether
family crisis intervention shortly after initial police contact
is more effective than traditional methods of dealing with
juvenile status and juvenile misdemeanor offenders. The
results of the counseling were found to be favorable.

---

362 Therrien, Mark E. Evaluating Empathy Skill
Training for Parents. Social Work, pp. 417-419,
September, 1979.

The results of this study indicated that parents who participated in PET training were able to function at facilita-
tive levels of empathy and that these skills were maintained over time.

---

363 Tramontana, Michael G., Sherrets, Steven D.,
and Authier, Karen. Evaluation of Parent Education Programs. Journal of Clinical Child Psychology 9(2):40-43, 1980.

Problems and issues involved in evaluating the effectiveness of parent education programs are examined, and
recent outcome research is reviewed. Three theoretical
approaches are involved in the program (parent effectiveness training, Adlerian concepts, and various behavior
principles), yet no conclusions are available on their comparative worth. Guidelines for remedying these difficulties in evaluation are suggested.

---

364 Whaler, R.G., and Fox, J.J. Solitary Toy Play
and Time Out: A Family Treatment Package for
Children with Aggressive and Oppositional Behavior. Journal of Applied Behavioral Analysis, pp.
23-29, Spring, 1980.

The behavior of four boys aged 5 to 8 who were referred
for a number of oppositional, rule-violating, and aggressive behaviors, was assessed by direct observation and

parental reports. Several Interventions were successively applied to each child's behavior. Changing the contract behavior to solitary toy play resulted in reduced oppositional behavior during the observation sessions, fewer reports from the parents of low-rate problem behaviors, and improvements in the parents' attitudes toward the children.

---

365 Waring, E.M. Family Therapy and Schizophrenia. Canadian Psychiatric Association Journal 23(1)51-58, 1978.

The author suggests that the empirical research on family influences in schizophrenia--particularly those factors which precipitate and perpetuate schizophrenic symptomatology--can be applied to evaluation of schizophrenics and their families and to specific family therapy with families of schizophrenics. It is suggested that evaluative research on the effectiveness of family therapy in schizophrenia will be necessary for family therapy to become more than a highly fascinating and experimental technique in the total management of schizophrenic patients.

---

366 Weathers, L., Liberman, L.P., and Coombs, R.H. Contingency Contracting with Families of Delinquent Adolescents. In: Behavior Theory and Practice--Annual Review, 1976, Vol. 4. New York: Brunner/Mazel, 1976.

A program of intensive, brief behavioral treatment was implemented with 28 male and female probationers and their families; no significant change was noted.

---

367 Wells, Richard A., and Dezen, Alan E. The Results of Family Therapy Revisited: The Nonbehavioral Methods. Family Process 17(3):251-274, 1978.

Studies from 1971 to 1976 reporting on the outcome of the nonbehavioral family therapies are analyzed and critically reviewed. Such research has increased in both quality and quantity since 1970. Particularly potent effects were noted for family therapy as an alternative to psychiatric hospitalization, with psychosomatic problems in children and adolescents, and in certain applications with parent-child and parent-adolescent relationships. However, a number of studies comparing family therapy with no formal treatment or an alternative treatment found little difference in outcome. Problems in family therapy outcome research are discussed.

---

368 Windell, James O., and Windell, Ellen A. Parent Group Training Programs in Juvenile Courts: A National Survey. Family Coordinator 26(4):459-463, 1977.

A fairly recent shift in focus toward the families of aggressive children has produced some group techniques for changing the behavior of such children. Data from 191 of 476 juvenile courts surveyed indicated that only one of five courts has a parent group program, and few use procedures reported in the growing literature relating to changing the behavior of aggressive children.

---

369 Witte, Frank Benedetto. Family Systems Perspective in Work with Juvenile Delinquents, Status Offenders, and Dependent Youth: Outcome and Process Evaluation of Training. Ph.D. Dissertation. Dissertation Abstracts International 40(6):2862-B, 1979.

In an outcome and process evaluation of training, juvenile justice intake counselors in four Florida judicial districts were given training in the theory and practice of family counseling from a family systems perspective. Counselors receiving training in the family systems perspective increased their levels of skill, knowledge, comfort, and effectiveness in family counseling. Counselors applied their knowledge and skills by reducing their use of formal court proceedings and increasing their counseling of juvenile delinquents, status offenders, and dependent youth.

---

*370 Woodward, C.A., et al. Aspects of Consumer
Satisfaction with Brief Family Therapy. Family
Process 17(4):399-407, 1978.*

In an evaluative study of brief family therapy, 279 families were administered a Family Satisfaction Questionnaire in their homes, 6 months after treatment was terminated. It assessed several aspects of the families' satisfaction with services received. The identified patient in all families was a child with academic and/or behavioral problems at school. Families were generally satisfied with the overall services received, but expressed widely varying degrees of satisfaction with various aspects of treatment.

---

*371 Woodward, C.A., et al. The Role of Goal
Attainment Scaling in Evaluating Family Therapy
Outcome. American Journal of Orthopsychiatry
48(3):464-476, 1978.*

The role of an individualized goal attainment procedure as an outcome measure for brief family therapy is described. Establishment of a scale and assessment of goal attainment at 6-month follow-up are reported in a study of some 270 families. Results support the procedure as being a reliable and valid means of examining the outcome status of treated families.

---

*372 Wunderlich, Richard A., Jewell, Lozes, and
Lewis, James. Recidivism Rates of Group Therapy
Participants and Other Adolescents Processed by a
Juvenile Court. Psychotherapy: Theory, Research,
and Practice 11(3):243-245, 1974.*

This paper describes a program of short-term group therapy for adolescent drug abusers and their parents that attempted to improve communication so that families would be better able to handle future conflicts. Demographic and recidivism data of the adolescent participants are compared with similar information from nondrug juvenile offenders.

---

373 Ziegler-Driscoll, Genevra. Family Research Study at Eagleville Hospital and Rehabilitation Center. Family Process 16:175-189, 1977.

The design of and recruitment for the Eagleville Hospital and Rehabilitation Center "Family Study Program" for low-income alcohol- or drug-dependent patients are described. Reasons for the high attrition rate included a prolonged interval between treatment and entry into the family study, lack of readiness of family members, and disenchantment with ongoing sessions.

---

374 Ziegler-Driscolla, Genevra. Similarities in Families of Drug Dependents and Alcoholics. New York: Gardner Press, 1979.

An Eagleville Center family study on the similarities between families of alcoholics and drug dependents is described. The 90 families studied had a similar distribution of family types, families of origin, and families of procreation.

Programs, Service Delivery, Training, and Supervision

The papers and publications cited in this section describe efforts to use family counseling in criminal justice, educational, medical, and social service settings at the organizational level. Programs and experiences in training and supervising personnel in the use of family counseling are also described.

---

375 Alexander, H., McQuiston, M., and Rodeheffer, M. *Residential Family Therapy*. In: *Abused Child--A Multidisciplinary Approach to Developmental Issues and Treatment*. Cambridge, Massachusetts: Ballinger Publishing, 1976.

This paper is a description of the residential therapy program for abusive families established in 1974 at the National Center for the Prevention and Treatment of Child Abuse in Denver.

---

376 Allen, James D., Jr. *Peer Group Supervision in Family Therapy*. Child Welfare 55(3):183-192, 1976.

This paper describes the 2-year experience of a group of social workers engaged in family therapy, who experimented with the use of peer-group supervision. It examines the theoretical and practical aspects of peer-group supervision.

---

377 Anderson, Linda M., Amatea, Elen S., Munson, Priscilla A., and Rudner, Becki A. *Training in Family Treatment: Needs and Objectives*. Social Casework 60(6):323-329, 1979.

An examination of the literature about family-oriented treatment in social work reveals that caseworkers' unfamiliarity with this mode of intervention has limited its use. An assessment of agency, worker, and family needs and resulting service-delivery objectives are presented, and an outline for a model training program is given.

---

378 Anderson, Lorna M., and Shafer, Gretchen. Family Sexual Abuse. American Journal of Ortho-psychiatry 49(3):436-445, 1979.

The authors present a collaborative approach to treating sexually abusive families, in which such families are viewed as analogous to "character-disordered" individuals. This model, unlike traditional voluntary treatment models, assumes that effective intervention requires authoritative control and careful coordination of all professional activity. Phases of treatment are outlined, and a case history is presented.

---

379 Anderson, P.S., et al. Family Crisis Intervention Program--Clark County, Washington. Washington, D.C.: U.S. Government Printing Office, 1979.

Described are the key features, functional characteristics, and organization of the Clark County, Washington, family crisis intervention unit which provides services to status offenders.

---

380 Bordill, Donald R. The Simulated Family as an Aid to Learning Family Group Treatment. Child Welfare 55(10):703-709, 1976.

Discusses the use of the simulated family technique for teaching principles of family group treatment to experienced and beginning therapists through intellectual, emotional, and active and passive modes of learning. Consideration is given to role-playing procedures, selection of players for family and therapist roles, formulation of the problem, the simulated interview, and debriefing.

---

381 Barnes, Geoffrey B., Chabon, Robert S., and Hertzberg, Leonard J. Team Treatment for Abusive Families. Social Casework 55(10):600-611, 1974.

The authors review pertinent historical problems leading to innovative approaches in the management of abusive families and discuss the experiences of a child abuse project in Sinai Hospital in Baltimore, Maryland. The team members view child abuse as a social ill, the roots of which often stem from an unhealthy environment within the family of the victim.

---

382 Berg, Berthold. *Learning Family Therapy Through Simulation. Psychotherapy: Theory, Research, and Practice 15(1):56-60D, 1978.*

A method was developed using simulated families in the training of family therapists. Students are given brief character sketches, role-play evaluation, and therapy by co-therapists while other students and the instructor serve as consultants.

---

383 Blomberg, T. G. *Accelerated Family Intervention in Juvenile Justice--An Exploration and a Recommendation for Constraint. Crime and Delinquency 25(4):497-502, 1979.*

The change in family intervention from an informal alternative in the treatment of juvenile offenders to a formal adjudicatory option is examined. A trend, illustrated by legislation passed in Florida, is discussed.

---

384 Bordill, Donald S. *The Simulated Family as an Aid to Learning Family Group Treatment. Child Welfare 55(10):703-711, 1976.*

Interest in family group treatment theory and methods has encouraged innovative teaching approaches. For example, the use of video and audio tapes in case studies and the student/experienced therapist cotherapy arrangement have proved valuable. This paper discusses the use of the simulated family in teaching concepts and principles of family group treatment.

---

385 Cautley, Patricia W. *Treating Dysfunctional Families at Home. Social Work 25(5):380-387, 1980.*

This article describes Project OPT, a program of short-term treatment for dysfunctional families. Stemming from the national interest in permanent planning for children, the project was formed to work with intact families at home to lessen the possibility of removing the children to foster care. The author describes the treatment methods used as well as measures of the project's effectiveness.

---

386 Chabot, David R.   Family Therapy with Court-Committed, Institutionalized, Acting-Out Male Adolescents.   Clinical Psychologist 29(4):8-9, 1976.

A family therapy service at a private residential treatment facility is described, in which about 90% of the parents who are invited to participate in family therapy agree to do so.

---

387 Churven, P. G.   Family Intervention for Beginners: A Rationale for a Brief Problem-Oriented Approach in Child and Family Psychiatry. Australia and New Zealand Journal of Psychiatry 13(3):235-239, 1979.

Many therapists in community health centers work with children and families but lack training and experience in resolving child/family problems. Inexperienced therapists often find the family therapy models described in the literature to be too complex. This paper describes a simplified view of family survival functions and a related problem-oriented intervention technique evolved for the training and supervision of community health workers.

---

388 Coleman, W.   Occupational Therapy and Child Abuse.   American Journal of Occupational Therapy 75(29):412-417, 1975.

This report describes the part occupational therapy played in a community-based research and demonstration project instituted to treat abusive parents and their children.

The psychosocial and psychological dynamics of abusive parents are reviewed.

---

389 Constantine, Larry L. Designed Experience: A Multiple, Goal-Directed Training Program in Family Therapy. Family Process 15(4):373-387, 1976.

A family therapy training program--one of three main branches of a Boston State hospital model--is discussed. Salient features of the program include planned integration of a multiplicity of experiential and cognitive learning modes; grounding in a unified, theoretical framework that is neither eclectic nor limited to a single school of thought; focus on non-pathological process in families; and systematic structuring in terms of specific, articulated, training objectives.

---

390 Cromwell, Ronald E., and Kenney, Bradford P. Diagnosing Marital and Family Systems: A Training Model. Family Coordinator 28(1):101-108, 1979.

A three-part training model is described. The first unit introduces an array of diagnostic tools and techniques. The second unit focuses on family systems theory and its relation to diagnosis. The third unit integrates the derived theory of diagnosing marital and family systems, termed "systemic diagnosis," with clinical application of diagnostic strategy with marital dyads and four-member families.

---

391 Daly, Liam. Family Violence: A Psychiatric Perspective. Journal of the Irish Medical Association 68(18):450-453, 1975.

Family violence is categorized into three types of interest to forensic psychiatrists: homicide, infanticide, and child or wife battering. The author recommends that a specialized team provide services for addressing family violence within the community.

135

392 Davenport, Patricia. How Should Families Be Involved in Service Delivery: A Public Agency's Point of View. In: Child Abuse and Neglect, Issues on Innovation and Implementation; Proceedings of the 2nd National Conference on Child Abuse and Neglect, April 17-20, 1977.

This paper stresses the need for formulating a flexible treatment plan in situations where a team approach to treating child abuse is not feasible and where the protective service worker handles all aspects of the case. It is suggested that the parents become involved in every aspect of the case.

---

393 Davis, Terry S., and Hagood, Linda A. Family Rehabilitation Coordinator Training for In-Home Recovery Assistance Services to Alcoholic Mothers, Their Children and Families. University of California, Los Angeles, Department of Continuing Education in Health Sciences, 1977.

This document contains background information on and the curriculum for the family rehabilitation counselor (FRC) training program developed in the NIAAA-supported FRC project at the University of California, Los Angeles (extension).

---

394 Fontana, V.J., and Robinson, E. Multidisciplinary Approach to the Treatment of Child Abuse. Pediatrics 57(5):760-764, 1976.

A team of professionals and paraprofessionals provide training for parents for improving parental responsiveness and decreasing social and environmental stress that can lead to child abuse. The two components of the program are a resident patient plan and an outpatient "I care" program.

---

395 Finkelstein, N.E. Family-Centered Group Care. Child Welfare 59(1):33-41, 1980.

Alternate frameworks for a model of residential group care focused on the family have the primary objective of early discharge from group care. The proposals are based on one agency's experience.

---

396 Fuller, Gordon M., and Pew, Wilmer L. *Family and Marriage Education "Recording." Individual Psychologist* 15(1):46-52, 1978.

A recording system is used at family and marriage education sessions of a community mental health program. The system was devised to help organize session content for purposes of recordkeeping, training, and refreshing counselors' memory prior to sessions. Students from family counseling and group counseling classes observe and record both marriage and family education sessions.

---

397 Garber, Howard L. *Bridging the Gap from Preschool to School for the Disadvantaged Child. School Psychology Digest* 8(3):303-310, 1979.

Early childhood education and its lack of success in solving the problems of disadvantaged preschoolers, as well as the various sources for the problems the children encounter in school, are discussed. Research is reported that supports providing a comprehensive rehabilitation program for the entire family rather than just for the preschooler.

---

398 Gershenson, J., and Cohen, M.S. *Through the Looking Glass: The Experiences of Two Family Therapy Trainees with Live Supervision. Family Process* 17(2):225-230, 1978.

A thorough investigation of the literature pertaining to therapy supervision reveals that supervision has never been examined from the viewpoint of the trainee. This paper examines live supervision of family therapy from that viewpoint. It suggests that live supervision is a powerful and effective tool--a tool that engenders a strong emotional response.

---

399 Guldner, Claude A. *Family Therapy for the Trainee in Family Therapy. Journal of Marriage and Family Counseling 4(1):127-132, 1978.*

The growth and self-understanding of the therapist as a person are considered by most training centers to be a significant part of the training process. This article reports on a pilot project that provided marital and family therapy for trainees in a 2-year program. Therapy was established on a contract basis and included individual, conjoint, family intergenerational, and small group therapies. Interns and family members responded favorably to the program. Supervisors found that the experience enabled trainees to maintain an experiential consistency with a general systems model utilized as the core theory of the training program.

---

400 Guttman, Herta A., and Sigal, John J. *Teaching Family Psychodynamics in a Family Practice Center: One Experience. International Journal of Psychiatry in Medicine 8(4):383-392, 1977-78.*

A method of teaching family psychodynamics in a new family practice center is described. Initially, there were difficulties in engaging staff because of inappropriate teaching methods and personal professional identify conflicts. Ultimately, a sequential program of video playbacks, live interviews, and case conferences was developed. The residents' rotation in psychiatry proved essential for developing a sense of feeling comfortable working with the psychological and familial aspects of physical illness.

---

401 Harbin, H.T. *A Family-Oriented Psychiatric Inpatient Unit. Family Process 18(3):281-291, 1979.*

This article presents the structure and policies of a psychiatric inpatient unit that was developed with the goal of fully integrating family-oriented treatment approaches into its therapeutic program. There is an explanation of different methods to involve families in the hospital treatment

process and delineation of a variety of treatment techniques specifically for families of inpatients. The role of
the nursing staff is described, as well as some of the
contradictions and paradoxes that are inherent in this
type of inpatient unit.

---

402 Hindman, Margaret.   Children of Alcoholic Parents.   Alcohol Health and Research World, pp. 2-6,
Winter, 1975-76.

This article reviews research, treatment approaches, and
intervention strategies related to problems experienced by
children of alcoholics. Alateen, family therapy, and
school-based interventions are highlighted as promising
approaches to treatment and prevention.

---

403 Horwitz, Arlene.   Treatment Program for Abused
Children and Their Families in Conjunction with
Nursing Education.   In: Child Abuse and Neglect,
Issues on Innovation and Implementation; Proceed-
ings of the 2nd National Conference on Child Abuse
and Neglect, April 17-20, 1977.

Since it is recognized that child abuse stems from conflict
in the home, the author states, it should also be recognized that intervention must take place within that system.
Nursing students are ideal therapists, since they are
seldom perceived as obstrusive authority figures.

---

404 Huberty, Catherine E., and Huberty, David J.
Treating the Parents of Adolescent Drug Abusers.
Contemporary Drug Problems 5(4):573-592, 1976.

A program for rehabilitating the marriages of parents of
drug-abusing youth is outlined. The family constellation
is explored by a family attribute analysis that defines
family roles and values. Supportive techniques include
encouragement, communication, permission giving, home-
work, married therapist couple as role models, and evaluation and referral.

---

405 Kiersh, E. Can Families Survive Incest? Cor-
rections Magazine 6(2):31-38, 1979.

Alternatives are discussed for preventing the commitment
of incestuous fathers to mental hospitals and prisons by
providing therapeutic treatment for the entire family and
by keeping the family unit intact.

---

*406 Kramer, Jerald N. Family Counseling as a Key
to Successful Alternative School Programs for
Alienated Youth. School Counselor 24(3):194-196,
1977.*

A family counseling program for alienated secondary
school students is described. The program is supervised
by the school principal and head counselor and is staffed
by certified family counselors trained in family therapy.
Evaluation is accomplished through counselor and client
assessment of progress on a continuing basis.

---

*407 Kuppersmith, Judith, Blair, Rima, and
Slotnick, Robert. Training Undergraduates as
Co-Leaders of Multifamily Counseling Groups.
Teaching of Psychology 4(1):3-6, 1977.*

A training program is described in which undergraduates
were prepared to serve as leaders of multi-family groups,
including delinquent youths, referred by the probation
department. Selection, training procedures, and benefits
of the program to students and families are described.

---

*408 Labate, Luciano, et al. Training Family Psy-
chologists: The Family Studies Program at Georgia
State University. Professional Psychology 10(1):
58-65, 1979.*

The authors describe a family studies program, which has
a two-phased clinical format that combines theory and
practice. The format is not fixed but will change as
knowledge in the field increases.

---

409 *LaBlang, Theodore R.   The Family Stress Con-*
sultation Team: An Illinois Approach to Protec-
tive Services.   Child Welfare 58(9):597-604, 1979.

An experimental, multidisciplinary approach to the
handling of child abuse and neglect cases is described.

---

410 *Liddle, Howard A.   The Emotional and Political*
Hazards of Teaching and Learning Family Therapy.
Family Therapy 5(1):1-12, 1978.

The sociopolitical impact of teaching and learning family
therapy in an intrapsychically oriented academic department is discussed. The author describes typical systemic
resistances to family therapy training and the usual
trainee resistances to learning this new viewpoint. Recommendations for dealing with such difficulties are offered
for both trainers and trainees.

---

411 *Littauer, Celia.   Working with Families of*
Children in Residential Treatment.   Child Welfare
59(4):225-234, 1980.

This article examines in detail the many ways in which
child care workers can work with families of children in
residential centers to facilitate early return home.

---

412 *McKamy, Ray L.   Multiple Family Therapy on an*
Alcohol Treatment Unit.   Family Therapy 3(3):197-
209, 1976.

The author traces the development of a multi-family treatment program in a hospital unit for alcoholics and
describes the experiences encountered by the therapists.
Principles of family therapy are discussed, and case
reports illustrating successful therapeutic techniques in
areas such as support, confrontation, interpretation, and
improvement in family communication are presented.

---

*413 Michaels, Kenneth W., and Green, Robert H.   A
Child Welfare Agency Project: Therapy for Families of Status Offenders.   Child Welfare 58(3):
216-220, 1979.*

Describes a project that was designed to deal with problem behaviors of juveniles and to reduce State and county
costs of placing the youths in institutions.   Family interaction is assessed, and the immediate problem is dealt
with through family therapy.

---

*414 Moroney, Robert M.   The Family as a Social
Service: Implications for Policy and Practice.
Child Welfare 57(4):211-220, 1978.*

The concept of the family as being in itself an important
social service suggests the need for policies based on the
interaction between families and other social institutions
providing services.   This view has important implications,
particularly in the care of handicapped persons.

---

*415 New Directions: the Family Center Youth Pro-
gram, Santa Barbara, California.   Human Relations
Center, Inc., 1979.*

The development and current status of the New Directions
Family Center Youth Program in Santa Barbara, California,
are discussed.   A family systems approach is used in
therapy that is based on the philosophy that alcoholism is
a family-centered problem.

---

*416 Ney, P.G., and Mills, W.A.   A Time-Limited
Treatment Program for Children and Their Families.
Hospital and Community Psychiatry 76(28):878-879,
1976.*

In 1972, the family psychiatric unit opened at Royal
Jubilee Hospital in Victoria for the treatment of children

under age 15 who have emotional disturbances or behavioral problems. Each child is admitted for 5 weeks, during which time the child's family is also involved in treatment. After the child is released from the unit, therapy continues for an additional 5 weeks in the family's home.

---

417 NSPCC Battered Child Research Team. At Risk: An Account of the Work of the Battered Child Research Department, NSPCC. London: Routledge and Kegan Paul, 1976.

This volume describes a total-family, multiple-modality approach to treatment of child abuse. Chapters consider the overall management of cases, protection of children, the primary therapeutic relationship, the use of professional and untrained workers, evaluation of progress, psychological aspects of battering parents, and characteristics of battered children.

---

418 Olson, U.J., and Pegg, P.E. Direct Open Supervision: A Team Approach. Family Process 15(4):463-469, 1980.

Created in the absence of one-way mirror facilities, "direct open supervision" combines elements of live supervision with team participation in training family therapists. The theory and application of this approach to direct supervision are described.

---

419 Palkon, Dennis S. Conjoint Alcohol Family Therapy Services for Occupational Alcoholism Programs. Labor-Management Alcoholism Journal 9(2): 55-62ff, 1979.

This paper analyzes the various treatment approaches in alcoholism, reviews the literature on conjoint alcohol family therapy (CAFT) and the effects of alcoholism on children, reviews the roles of labor and management in regard to conjoint services, offers pragmatic recommendations for implementing CAFT services, and discusses the limitations and the benefits of conjoint approaches in alcoholism.

---

*420 Raasoch, J., and Laqueur, H.P.   Learning Mul-
tiple Family Therapy Through Simulated Workshops.
Family Process 18(1):95-98, 1979.*

Multiple Family Therapy (MFT) can be learned more
rapidly through simulated workshops. A chronological
approach to a simulated workshop is outlined describing
mechanics and techniques. The hardest parts of simulated and real MFT are "taking off" and "landing." Specific exercises are detailed to facilitate the early phases
when professionals tend to simulate excessive psychopathology. However, recovery is usually rapid and dramatic
in simulations.

---

*421 Roth, R.A.   Multidisciplinary Teams in Child
Abuse and Neglect Programs: A Special Report from
the National Center on Child Abuse and Neglect.
Washington, D.C.:   National Center on Child Abuse
and Neglect, 1978.*

The growing use of multidisciplinary teams for child abuse
intervention and treatment, types of teams used, and
methods of operation are summarized in this document. A
list of programs using this approach is appended.

---

*422 Schneiderman, G., and Pakes, E.G.   The Teach-
ing of Family Therapy Skills on an In-Patient
Child Psychiatry Ward.   Family Therapy 3(1):29-33,
1976.*

This article discusses the teaching and application of family therapy skills to the parapsychiatric staff of an inpatient child psychiatric ward. A case history illustrates a
family transactional model which has enhanced the therapeutic activity of the ward.

---

*423 Schulman, Gerda L.   Teaching Family Therapy to
Social Work Students.   Social Casework 57(7):448-
459, 1976.*

The teaching of family therapy is illustrated by combining
experience with the traditional didactic approach in an

144

academic setting. Tools include material from students'
life experience and casework, audio and video tapes, and
role playing, including dramatization of family scenes.
Especially important is the live family demonstration interview, with the instructor serving as the family consultant.

---

*424 Shyne, Ann W., and Neuman, Renee. Commitment
to People: An Evaluation of the Family Reception
Center. New York: Child Welfare League of
Amerca, 1974.*

This center is a multiservice, neighborhood-based program
established to keep families together. Service components
of the center include crisis-oriented counseling through
individual and family casework and sustained family group
therapy.

---

*425 Sigal, John J., and Levin, Sol. Teaching Fam-
ily Therapy by Simulation. Canada's Mental Health
24(2):6-8, 1976.*

The use of simulation permits trainees to experience per-
sonally the effect on families or individuals of different
approaches to dealing with problems, and to witness the
consequences for such problems by therapeutic maneuvers.

---

*426 Sprenkle, Douglas H., and Fisher, Barbara L.
Family Therapy Conceptualization and Use of Case
Notes. Family Therapy 5(2):177-183, 1978.*

A method of case conceptualization is presented, based on
the writing of meaningful case notes. While both the conceptual scheme and the case notes form were designed for
trainees at the Purdue Marriage and Family Counseling
Center, they have also proven useful for experienced
therapists.

---

*427 Stedman, James M., and Gaines, Thomas.
Trainee Response to Family Therapy Training. Family Therapy 5(1):81-90, 1978.*

Similarities between staff-trainers and trainees were investigated in terms of their distribution of concepts/persons during 100 family evaluations. Results show that although all trainees did differ significantly from staff, there was a tendency for longer-term trainees to become more like staff over time.

---

428 Stollery, P.L.   Searching for the Magic Answer to Juvenile Delinquency.   Washington, D.C.: Administrative Office of the United States Court, 1977.

A community-based program for juvenile delinquents and their families is described which incorporates the delivery of appropriate clinical services within an authoritative and coercive framework.   The program incorporates group and family therapy in which the counselor acts as a directive parental figure.

---

429 Teicher, Joseph D., Sinay, Ruth, and Stumphauzer, Jerome S.   Training Community-Based Paraprofessionals as Behavior Therapists with Families of Alcohol-Abusing Adolescents.   American Journal of Psychiatry 133(7):846-850, 1976.

A pilot program was established in California to train 10 paraprofessionals to conduct behavioral family therapy in the homes of alcohol-abusing adolescents.   It is concluded that this program is a viable model for training paraprofessionals.

---

430 Tomm, K.M., and Wright, L.M.   Training in Family Therapy: Perceptual, Conceptual, and Executive Skills.   Family Process 18(3):227-250, 1979.

This paper presents a comprehensive and detailed outline of family therapy skills to aid in providing a more precise focus in the training of family therapy clinicians.   The skills are based on an integrated treatment model within a systems framework.   Four major functions performed by a

146

family therapist are separated and are further differentiated into general therapeutic competencies. Specific perceptual, conceptual, and executive skills are described in the form of instructional objectives and are listed under each competency.

---

431 Tucker, Bernice Z., and Liddle, Howard A.
*Intra-and Interpersonal Process in the Group
Supervision of Family Therapists.* Family Therapy
5(1):13-27, 1978.

The outcomes of a specific model of group supervision and the details of some of the effects of this training on 10 doctoral-level trainees are discussed. The supervision model involved live observation of family therapy sessions by the student group and the supervisor, and post-session group discussions of therapy techniques and family interactions. The practicum experience resulted in the development of therapeutic skills and in the growth of the trainee/therapists as persons.

---

432 U.S. Department of Health and Human Services.
*Helping Youth and Families of Separation, Divorce,
and Remarriage: A Program Manual.* Washington,
D.C.:   U.S. Government Printing Office, 1980.

This document is designed to help program planners and service providers who wish to expand current services or to develop new social and support services for families experiencing problems that are associated with family transitions (separation, divorce, or remarriage). It provides a discussion of the family counseling model, and details how this model can be specifically applied to divorce and remarriage.

---

433 Viaro, M.   Case Report: Smuggling Family
Therapy Through. Family Process 19(1):35-44,
1980.

Therapists with a family systems orientation are, on occasion, called upon to work in settings where political constraint, cultural patterns, or the unchangeable expectations of the clinical population make it impossible to identify the treatment as being directed at the family. Under these circumstances, family therapy concepts and techniques may be employed by smuggling them in under another label. This article describes a setting in which such a strategy was necessary.

---

434 Weingerten, K. *Family Awareness for Nonclinicians: Participation in a Simulated Family as a Teaching Technique. Family Process 18(2):143-150, 1979.*

This paper describes a course in family theory geared to "well" family members that combines didactic and experiential teaching techniques. A key feature of the course is that students participate in a simulated family for 12 weeks. Family therapists are skilled at using techniques that powerfully dramatize family process; they can provide a needed and useful service to the community by teaching the dynamics of family functioning to people who have a personal or professional interest in learning more about families.

---

435 Weissman, Harold H. *Integrating Services for Troubled Families: Dilemmas of Program Design and Implementation. San Francisco: Jossey-Bass, 1978.*

A social history of the development of the Lower East Side Family Union in New York City--a project initiated and designed to prevent the need for child placement through the integration and coordination of other agencies' services, as well as through the direct provision of social services.

---

436 Wertheimer, Dror. *Family Therapy Training in Israel. Journal of Marriage and Family Counseling 4(2):83-90, 1978.*

Some of the specific difficulties and features of training family therapists in a developing country are described, using Israel as an example. Many of Israel's families grew up in a completely different culture, have a different family structure, and are in the midst of a strenuous acculturation process into a Western democracy and a modern technological society. Nevertheness, the training of social workers as family therapists has shown promising results.

Prevention
and Education

Most of the annotations contained in this section of the bibliography focus on the prevention of pathological conditions in families or on enhancing positive family life. In some ways, these publications indicate the extent to which current knowledge about families has spread and been adopted in the Nation.

---

437 Abidin, Richard R. Parent Education and Intervention Handbook. Springfield, Illinois: Charles C Thomas, 1980.

Topics discussed in this handbook include developmental psychology as it relates to parenting; intervention strategies for parents of aggressive, hyperactive, learning disabled, abused or neglected, emotionally disturbed, or handicapped children; black parents; parents of preschool children; behavioral parenting; and training.

---

438 Abidin, Richard R. Parenting Skills: Trainer's Manual. New York: Human Sciences Press, 1979.

This book presents a program of "parenting skills sessions," which can provide parents with a working knowledge of the newer information accumulated by the various professions concerned with child development. The program also provides a chance for parents to develop and practice new skills based on this new knowledge.

---

439 Abidin, R.R. Parenting Skills Workbook. New York: Human Services Press, 1976.

The sessions that comprise this program represent an amalgamation of a wide range of educational strategies and theoretical orientations; among these are client-centered humanistic psychology, rational emotive psychology, and behavioral psychology. Each session presents skills that are effective in managing and changing behaviors of adults and children.

---

440 Arnold, L. Eugene. Helping Parents Help Their Children. New York: Brunner/Mazel, 1978.

This book covers the following topics: general principles of parent guidance; conceptual options in parent guidance; helping parents cope with specific problems of children; guiding parents who have specific problems; and guidance by professionals outside the mental health field. The book is practicé-oriented.

---

441 Arshack, S., ed. Child Abuse: Where Do We Go From Here? Conference Proceedings, February 18-20, 1977. Washington: Children's Hospital National Medical Center, 1977.

Six aspects of child abuse, ranging from causes and forms of child abuse to needs for court reform in handling of abuse cases, are covered by the papers contained in this volume. Prevention techniques and therapy for both parents and child are discussed in the section on treatment modalities.

---

442 Carrol, Nancy A., and Reich, John W. Issues in the Implementation of the Parent Aide Concept. Social Casework 59(3):152-160, 1978.

The authors describe the successful training and use of parents to visit and offer empathic support to child-abusing parents.

---

443 Clark, W. A. Approaches to Rural Juvenile Delinquency Prevention--Annual Report, July 1, 1977-June 30, 1978. Washington, D. C.: U. S. Department of Justice, 1978.

The first-year programs, activities, and efforts are featured of the Tuskegee Institute youth services program staff to reduce juvenile delinquency in selected Alabama communities. Family "counseling" efforts are described.

---

444 Coleman, S.B. *Sib Group Therapy: A Prevention Program for Siblings from Drug-Addicted Families.* International Journal of the Addictions 13(1):115-127, 1978.

To prevent drug abuse among younger siblings of addicted adolescents, weekly group therapy sessions were implemented at a suburban therapeutic drug community. The concept evolved as an outgrowth of family therapy which revealed that intergenerational addictive patterns might impose a high future risk of similar behavior among latency-age children. Results indicate that underlying psychodynamics appear somewhat unchanged.

---

445 Daugelli, Judy F., and Weener, Joan M. *Training Parents as Mental Health Agents.* Community Mental Health Journal 14(21):14-25, 1978.

The utilization of parents as mental health agents for their children is a service delivery strategy likely to have major impact on enhancement of normal families. Parents were introduced to the concepts and behavior skills of empathic responding, giving "I" messages, anticipatory structuring, limit setting, and modeling for preferred behaviors.

---

446 Denicola, Joseph, and Sandler, Jack. *Training Abusive Parents in Child Management and Self-Control Skills.* Behavior Therapy 11(2):263-270, 1980.

Effects of parent training and self-control techniques with child-abusing parents are examined in this paper. The children revealed an increase in pro-social, and less aversive, behavior during treatment and follow-up. The efficacy of teaching abusive parents anger-control techniques is discussed.

---

447 Fantini, Marion D., and Cardenas, Rene, eds. *Parenting in a Multicultural Society.* New York: Longman, 1980.

The authors in this anthology analyze viable forms of child training within a multicultural society. Families from black-American, Mexican-American, Puerto Rican, and other ethnic groups are examined. In addition, changes in family composition and the subsequent modifications in nurturing and providing for children are discussed.

---

448 Feldman, H. S. *Family Therapy: Its Role in the Prevention of Criminality.* Journal of Forensic Science 25(1):15-19, 1980.

The family imprints its members with selfhood in all cultures. Absence of family imprints can result in the development of deviant childhood behavior and loss of identity. If deterrents, namely poverty, and lack of family authority figures, rejection of the individual child, absence of family cohesiveness, and loss of individual identity within the family, were altered in their development by family therapy techniques, then criminal and deviant behavior would be decreased.

---

449 Gordon, Ira J. *Parent Education and Parent Involvement: Retrospect and Prospect.* Childhood Education 54(2):71-79, 1977.

The historical development of parent education programs in Europe and the United States are reviewed. Three models (family, school, and community impact) for parent education programs are discussed, along with the positive and negative aspects of each model. It is argued that efforts in all three models need to continue and be enlarged.

---

450 Gordon, Marlene. *Learning for Living: A Program Prepared for Use in a Group Home for Children: Leader's Guide.* New York: Salvation Army, 1978.

This report describes an Education for Parenthood demonstration program developed by the Salvation Army for teenagers. Weekly sessions, held over a 6-month period, emphasized self-esteem, knowledge about children, and career development in the child care field.

---

451 Gordon, T. *Effectiveness Training--A Model for Prevention of Juvenile Crime. Crime Prevention Review 4(1):20-25, 1976.*

The author advocates the use of parent effectiveness training (PET) as a way of dealing with one cause of juvenile crime, delinquency, and anti-social behavior-- namely, poor parent-child behavior patterns.

---

452 Helfer, R.E. *Child Abuse: A Plan for Prevention. Chicago: National Committee for Prevention of Child Abuse, 1978.*

Modifications in the delivery of health care services and educational systems are proposed in order to prevent major and frequent breakdowns in the interaction between parents and their children. The program's aid is to develop patterns of healthy interaction with the baby based on expert knowledge of the parenting skills and behavior most nurturing for the baby's emotional and physical health. This program would involve including public education courses that teach interpersonal skills appropriate for the specific age group being taught.

---

453 Holmes, Sally. *Parents Anonymous: A Treatment Method for Child Abuse. Social Work 23(3): 245-247, 1978.*

This article discusses Parents Anonymous of Michigan, which sets up groups in which helping professionals and abusive families cooperate. It differs from the usual group model in that members undergo treatment in chapters defined as groups, consisting of two to ten parents, led by a parent "chairperson," but therapeutically directed by a professional "sponsor."

---

454 Howard, Don, and Howard, Nancy. *Approach to Problem Drinking: A Four-Week Family Forum.* *Family Training Center, Columbia, Missouri.*

A manual for a four-week family forum is presented, including discussion material, reading assignments, and suggested exercises, with the objective of increasing knowledge and understanding of problem drinking and its effects on the alcoholic and the family. Emphasis is placed upon sharing of knowledge and experience and for exploring alternate ways of communicating.

---

455 Jason, Leonard. *Paraprofessionals Providing Behavioral Techniques to Families of Disadvantaged Toddlers.* *Exceptional Child 22(3):153-158, 1975.*

Family members were trained in a behavioral program designed to prevent disadvantaged toddlers evidencing early developmental lag from encountering subsequent cognitive, motivational, perceptual, and linguistic difficulties.

---

456 Jensen, Richard E. *A Behavioral Modification Program to Remediate Child Abuse.* *Journal of Clinical Child Psychology 5(1):30-32, 1976.*

On the assumption that child abuse is contributed to by parents' lack of effective child management skills, training in behavioral principles were developed for abusing parents.

---

457 Kruger, Lois, et al. *Group Work with Abuse Parents.* *Social Work 24(4):337-338, 1979.*

The need for additional services for abusive or neglectful parents in a community in Kansas City, Kansas, led graduate students in a social work practicum at the State Social and Rehabilitation Service to develop parent education group sessions, to instruct parents in alternative methods for disciplining children.

---

458 Lerman, Saf. *Parent Awareness Training: Positive Parenting for the 1980's. New York: A & W Publishers, 1979.*

This book describes a new, flexible technique of general child care in a question-and-answer format.

---

459 Lopata, Helena Znaniecki. *Family Factbook. Chicago University, 1978.*

This family factbook seeks to provide interesting and useful materials in areas that relate to the family primarily in the United States, although some mention is made of practices in other countries. Child development, day care, child abuse, and adolescents are discussed. Articles on the importance of good health care for children and family therapy in alcoholism are included.

---

460 Maybanks, Sheila, and Bryce, Marvin, eds. *Home-Based Services for Children and Families: Policy, Practice, and Research. Springfield, Illinois: Charles C Thomas, 1979.*

The editors present a series of articles addressing the implications of the practice of home-based services for children and families on several levels. The book begins with a call for the implementation of preventive programs and a simultaneous study of coping families, to develop models of prevention.

---

461 McLain, G.B. *Prevention and/or Treatment of Child Abuse and Neglect in Head Start--an Eclectic, Ecologic Hypothesis. Washington, D.C.: U.S. Department of Health and Human Services, 1978.*

The role of Head Start in preventing child abuse and neglect by integrating pre-school children into a comprehensive child development program and pre-school classes is considered. Head Start furnishes access to family therapy services.

---

462 McLaughlin, Clara J. *The Black Parents' Handbook: A Guide to Healthy Pregnancy, Birth and Child Care. New York: Harcourt, Brace, Jovanovich, 1976.*

This book discusses many aspects of parenthood--from the period of conception until the child is 6 years of age. Facts parents need to know are presented, and some medical problems are discussed, in addition to the cultural and psychological stresses to which black parents and children are subject.

---

463 Moses, Donald A., and Burger, Robert E. *Are You Driving Your Children to Drink? Coping with Teenage Alcohol and Drug Abuse. New York: Van Nostrand Reinhold, 1975.*

The problem of alcohol and drug abuse is seen as a symptom of a more malignant, underlying emotional disease caused by the disintegration of the family structure. An unstable parent/child relationship is cited as the single most important factor leading to addiction. The effects of disruptive family situations, compounded by social pressures, adolescent search for security, and peer relationships are explored.

---

464 National Institute on Drug Abuse. *A Family Response to the Drug Problem. Washington, D.C., U.S. Government Printing Office, 1976.*

This volume is based on a National Institute on Drug Abuse training program entitled <u>Families Involved in Nurture and Development</u>. Areas covered include an examination of the family's role in a modern society, evolution of family values, and how families make choices.

---

465 Rosenstein, Paula J. *Family Outreach: A Program for the Prevention of Child Neglect and Abuse. Child Welfare 57(9):519-526, 1978.*

The author describes a Texas volunteer program, which was designed to prevent child neglect and abuse, and also stresses promotion of the public's awareness of its responsibility to report suspected cases.

---

466 Schneiderman, Irene. *Family Thinking in Prevention of Alcoholism.* Preventive Medicine, Vol. 4, pp. 296-309, 1975.

Alcoholism prevention through family therapy is suggested as a possible mechanism for breaking the generational transmission chain of alcohol abuse. Evidence that alcoholism is familial is reviewed in terms of physiological predisposition and family structure. The concepts of family thinking and family therapy as they apply to alcoholic families are discussed.

---

467 Seidmon, Betty L. *Out of My Practice: The Marriage, Family, and Child Counselor and Public Education.* Marriage and Family Counselors Quarterly 12(4):47-49, 1978.

Ways of gaining public support and recognition for marriage, family, and child counselors through participation in public education are discussed. Workshop classes in parent training programs designed and taught by counselors are suggested. In addition, marriage, family, and child counselors can share skills in educating the public about child abuse, wife abuse, truancy, divorce crisis, and family therapy. It is proposed that counselors create programs of public training and seek a place in public education to encourage better mental health for individuals and families as a continuing process.

---

468 *Tender Loving Care: A Program Prepared for Mother-Baby and Maternity Centers of the Salvation Army: Leader's Guide.* New York: Salvation Army, 1976.

This guide, one of a series of Education for Parenthood manuals developed for use in Salvation Army demonstration programs, outlines a course for pregnant teenagers and teenage mothers in residential centers. The curriculum covers three aspects of parenthood: medical (including prenatal care, delivery, postnatal and infant care, and nutrition), physical-education (including housing, food, clothing, educational training, employment opportunities, and child care arrangements), and social-psychological (including child development, parent effectiveness, discipline, relationships, and dynamics of family life).

---

469 Turner, Charlene. *Resources for Help in Parenting. Child Welfare 59(3):179-188, 1980.*

This paper provides and briefly describes some sources of parenting information that may be useful to parents, educators, and human service personnel.

---

470 *U.S. Department of Health and Human Services, National Center on Child Abuse and Neglect. Overview of the Parents Anonymous Self-Help for Child Abusing Parents Project Evaluation Study for 1974-1976. Tucson, Arizona: Behavior Associates, 1977.*

An evaluation overview is presented of the Parents Anonymous project, which is designed to expand the self-help treatment approach for abusing parents and to aid agencies in their efforts to treat child abuse. The Parents Anonymous project provided information, consultation, and technical assistance to agencies and communities attempting to understand and remedy the problems of child abuse.

Key Word Index
and Index of Titles

Key Word Index

Action-Oriented Family Therapy--155.
Active-Directive Therapy--11.
Adaptability and Adaptation--47, 65, 259.
Addictions--See Alcohol Abuse and Alcoholism; Drug
    Abuse and Addiction.
Adlerian Concepts and Approaches--353, 363.
APGAR Scale--259.
Al-Anon--86, 109.
Alateen--109, 402.
Alcohol Abuse and Alcoholism--8, 31, 53, 56, 65, 76, 85,
    86, 98, 99, 101, 105, 109, 111, 116, 119, 127, 128,
    130, 131, 133, 135, 158, 162, 170, 178, 179, 197,
    209, 212, 229, 238, 256, 257, 262, 265, 267, 282,
    288, 289, 309, 312, 320, 322, 323, 324, 327, 340,
    343, 344, 352, 357, 358, 359, 373, 374, 393, 412,
    415, 419, 429, 454, 459, 463, 466.
Adolescence--See Juvenile Delinquency; Youth.
Alcoholics Anonymous--86, 99, 109.
American Indians--See Indians, American.
Angel, Family--148.
Anger and Anger Control Skills--85, 160, 446.
Asthma--332.
Attachment Theory--5, 30.
Balance Therapy--113.
Battering--See Child Abuse; Violence in the Family.
Behavior Modification--See Behavioral Therapy and
    Behavior Modification.
Behavioral Contracting--250.
Behavioral Marriage Therapy--24, 25, 317. Also see
    Marriage and Marital Therapy.
Behavioral Therapy and Behavior Modification--2, 19, 66,
    74, 75, 76, 94, 161, 177, 178, 179, 243, 250, 263,
    273, 290, 301, 302, 320, 329, 349, 363, 366, 429,
    437, 439, 445, 455, 456.
Blacks, Therapy with and/or Training for--134, 155, 156,
    157, 207, 208, 210, 228, 437, 447, 462.
Bonding Failure--59, 308.
Brief Focal Family Therapy--See Focal Family Therapy.
Case Conceptualization--426.
Case Notes--426.
Character-Disordered Family, The--67.
Charting--177.

Child Abuse--83, 89, 147, 176, 190, 203, 206, 211, 233,
     246, 253, 279, 286, 287, 308, 331, 375, 381, 388,
     391, 392, 394, 403, 409, 417, 421, 437, 441, 442,
     446, 452, 453, 456, 457, 459, 461, 465, 467, 470.
Children--9, 40, 46, 84, 92, 115, 121, 137, 143, 149,
     155, 156, 160, 161, 172, 189, 195, 199, 202, 215,
     219, 222, 223, 227, 232, 233, 242, 244, 245, 251,
     264, 269, 271, 272, 278, 301, 302, 314, 315, 328,
     330, 332, 333, 335, 336, 338, 340, 364, 367, 370,
     385, 387, 397, 402, 411, 413, 416, 422, 435, 437,
     438, 439, 440, 446, 447, 448, 449, 450, 451, 452,
     453, 455, 456, 457, 459, 460, 461, 462, 463, 465,
     467, 468.   Also see Child Abuse.
Children of Alcoholics--340, 393, 402, 419.
Circumplex Model--47, 348.
Client-Centered Family Therapy--11, 42, 43, 329.
Cohesion--47.
Collections, Papers in--26.
Communication Theory--24.
Community of Life Cycles, Concept of--229.
Community Treatment Model for Use in Sexual Abuse--67.
Conditioning--28, 179.
Conflict Management--59.
Conflict Resolution Model--40, 353.
Conflict Theory--58.
Confrontation--44, 209.
Conjoint Family Therapy--2, 13, 19, 87, 111, 122, 234,
     307, 347, 399, 419.   Also see Multiple Family
     Therapy.
Conjoint Hospitalization--111.
Conjoint Marital Therapy--306, 359.
Conjoint Therapy--107, 111, 168, 183.
Contracts, Marital--239, 248.
Contracts in Therapy--146, 152, 247, 250, 255, 268, 366.
Corrections--See Criminal Behavior, the Criminal Justice
     System, and Corrections.
Costs, Program--214, 301, 413.
Co-Therapy--107, 165, 192, 219, 235, 404.
Court Reform--441.
Criminal Behavior, the Criminal Justice System, and
     Corrections--14, 18, 35, 173, 175, 184, 214, 253,
     255, 258, 262, 268, 275, 277, 281, 283, 284, 294,
     295, 297, 298, 300, 310, 311, 326, 334, 346, 352,
     361, 366, 369, 372, 383, 405, 441, 443, 448, 451.

Also see Child Abuse; Juvenile Delinquency; Violence
in the Family.
Crisis Intervention--38, 40, 51, 90, 97, 105, 118, 230,
240, 253, 261, 269, 273, 298, 361, 379.
Crisis Intervention Model--40, 118.
Crisis-Oriented Counseling--73, 424.
Cubans, Therapy with--270. Also see Hispanics, Therapy
with.
Cybernetics--37.
Day Care--459.
Decentering--264.
Delayed Stress Response Syndrome--126.
Delinquency, Juvenile--See Juvenile Delinquency.
Denied Affects--87.
Dependency--90, 129, 198.
Depression--6.
Developmental Theory and Practice--45, 117, 276.
Diagnosis--16, 26, 37, 78, 182, 204, 223, 244, 347, 390.
Also see Evaluation, Client and/or Therapy; Inter-
viewing; Scales.
Direct Open Supervision--418.
Divorce--6, 160, 432, 467.
Dominance--235.
Double Binding--177, 285.
Drawings, Family Systems--285.
Dream Analysis--78.
Drop-Outs--373.
Drug Abuse and Addiction--60, 68, 76, 105, 110, 139,
159, 163, 165, 166, 167, 178, 179, 180, 185, 221,
234, 255, 261, 262, 281, 282, 293, 303, 304, 319,
321, 327, 341, 354, 355, 372, 373, 374, 404, 444,
463, 464.
Drugs, Pharmacological Use of--316.
Dyscontrol, Episodic--150.
Ecological Structural Family Therapy--270.
Ecostructural Family Therapy--100.
Ecosystemic Epistemology--37.
Education--13, 42, 106, 122, 216, 230, 272, 349, 353,
396, 397, 403, 434, 437, 449, 450, 452, 454, 457,
468.
Empathy Skill Training--362.
Equilibrium Theory--58.
Erickson, Eric--229.
Erickson, Milton H.--28.

Healthy Families and Family Characteristics--3, 45, 183, 200. Also see Normal Families, Research with.

Heroin Addiction--60. Also see Drug Abuse and Addiction.

High Impact Family Therapy--69, 277.

Hispanics, Therapy with--238, 270, 447.

History of Family Therapy--See Family Therapy, History of.

Home, Treatment and Research in the--155, 161, 194, 266, 285, 393, 416, 429, 460.

Home Observation Assessment Method--266.

Homeostasis--10, 30, 40, 49, 60, 128, 166, 260, 265, 285.

Homicide--298, 391.

Hospital Staff--151, 205, 401.

Humanistic Family Therapy Model--190.

Humanistic Psychology--145, 439.

Hypnosis--28, 55, 76.

Illness, Physical--200, 271, 332, 400. Also see Health and Medical Care.

Immigrants, Therapy with--100, 270.

Incest--145, 254, 405.

Indians, American--117.

Infanticide--391.

Inpatient Treatment and Residential Care--14, 76, 91, 92, 111, 151, 159, 161, 189, 197, 205, 209, 226, 269, 303, 321, 322, 350, 359, 375, 386, 394, 395, 401, 411, 412, 416, 422, 468.

Intergenerational Addiction Patterns--444.

Intergenerational Issues and Therapy--See Multigenerational Issues and Therapy.

Intergenerational Separation Anxiety--199.

Internalization--220.

Interpersonal Distance--330.

Interviewing--94, 102, 149, 157, 202, 217, 314, 345, 347, 380, 400, 423. Also see Diagnosis; Evaluation, Client and/or Therapy.

Intimacy--191.

Involuntary Clients (Court-Ordered Therapy)--175.

Irish Families--101.

Israel--436.

Jackson, Don D.--19.

Juvenile Delinquency--18, 35, 38, 66, 69, 73, 96, 173, 174, 175, 184, 233, 241, 268, 275, 277, 279, 284, 290, 291, 292, 294, 295, 297, 299, 300, 310, 326, 329, 334, 337, 338, 361, 366, 368, 369, 372, 383,

386, 407, 413, 428, 443, 451. Also see Alcohol and
Alcoholism; Children; Drug Abuse and Addiction;
Parents, Parenting, Parental Therapy, and Parents'
Training; Youth.
Kinetic Psychotherapy--251.
Labeling Theory--20.
Literature Reviews--14, 61, 65, 68, 158, 159, 170, 185,
200, 208, 260, 262, 286, 293, 319, 323, 324, 335,
352, 354, 357, 367, 377, 398.
Live Consultation--95.
Live Supervision--398, 418.
Low-Income Families--100, 132, 134, 245, 373.
Mapping, Relationship--106, 113.
Marriage and Marital Therapy--2, 15, 22, 47, 53, 54, 57,
65, 69, 70, 85, 86, 88, 98, 101, 111, 113, 116, 138,
144, 156, 165, 166, 168, 183, 190, 199, 211, 213,
235, 239, 247, 248, 249, 264, 265, 278, 306, 318,
322, 343, 346, 348, 359, 390, 391, 396, 399, 404,
432, 367. Also see Behavioral Marriage Therapy.
Men--235, 309.
Mexican Americans--447. Also see Hispanics, Therapy
with.
Minorities, Therapy for--46. Also see Blacks, Therapy
and/or Training for; Hispanics, Therapy with;
Indians, American.
Multicultural Society, Parenting in--447.
Multidisciplinary Treatment and Training--131, 375, 394,
409, 421.
Multigenerational Issues and Therapy--101, 137, 138, 142,
233, 307, 399.
Multiple Couples Therapy--155. Also see Conjoint Family
Therapy; Conjoint Marital Therapy; Conjoint
Therapy; Multiple Family Therapy.
Multiple Family Therapy--14, 61, 82, 134, 180, 209, 407,
412, 420. Also see Conjoint Family Therapy;
Conjoint Marital Therapy; Conjoint Therapy; Multiple
Couples Therapy.
Multiple Impact Family Therapy--210.
Multiple Personalities--77.
Multiple Therapists--69, 227. Also see Conjoint Family
Therapy; Conjoint Couples Therapy; Conjoint Marital
Therapy; Conjoint Therapy; Co-Therapy;
Tri-Therapist Team.
Multiproblem Families--97, 137.

Index of Titles

The following index contains an alphabetical listing of the titles of the publications described in this book. The numbers in parentheses following titles refer to the number assigned to each title in the preceding bibliography.

Abstinence or Control: The Outcome for Excessive Drinkers Two Years After Consultation. (344)

Accelerated Family Intervention in Juvenile Justice--An Exploration and a Recommendation for Constraint. (383)

Action-Oriented Family Therapy. (155)

Adolescence, Delinquency, and Family--Experiences from Family Therapy. (292)

Alcoholics Anonymous and Family Therapy. (109)

Alcoholism as Viewed Through Family Systems Theory and Family Psychotherapy. (8)

Alcoholism Treatment Services for Children of Alcoholics. (340)

Alcoholism. (343)

Alcoholism: A Controlled Trial of "Treatment" and "Advice." (309)

Alcoholism: A Family Systems Approach. (133)

Alcoholism: Illness or Problem in Interaction. (312)

Alderscage Youth Service Bureau--Family Counseling Approach to Delinquent Youth--Self-Assessment Report, January 1, 1976-December 31, 1976. (281)

Annual Review of Family Therapy. (6)

Application of the Basic Principles of Family Therapy to the Treatment of Drug and Alcohol Abusers. (178)

Approach to Problem Drinking: A Four-Week Family
Forum. (454)

Approaches to Rural Juvenile Delinquency Prevention--
Annual Report, July 1, 1977-June 30, 1978. (443)

Are You Driving Your Children to Drink? Coping with
Teenage Alcohol and Drug Abuse. (463)

Aspects of Consumer Satisfaction with Brief Family
Therapy. (370)

At Risk: An Account of the Work of the Battered Child
Research Department, NSPCC. (417)

Attachment Theory, Object-Relations Theory, and Family
Therapy. (5)

Becoming a Family Therapist. (188)

Behavior Therapy in a Family Context: Treating Elective
Mutism. (242)

Behavior Therapy Strategies as Applied to Family
Therapy. (263)

Behavioral Contracting: Theory and Design. (250)

Behavioral Marriage Therapy: I. A Psychodynamic-
Systems Analysis and Critique. (24)

Behavioral Marriage Therapy: II. Empirical
Perspective. (317)

Behavioral Marriage Therapy: IV. Take Two Aspirin and
Call Us in the Morning. (25)

A Behavioral Modification Program to Remediate Child
Abuse. (456)

Behavioral Treatment of Marital Discord. (2)

The Black Parents' Handbook: A Guide to Healthy
Pregnancy, Birth and Child Care. (462)

Bridging the Gap from Preschool to School for the Disadvantaged Child. (397)

Brief Family Therapy for Childhood Tic Syndrome. (271)

Brief Focal Family Therapy When the Child Is the Referred Patient: I. Clinical. (84)

Brief Focal Family Therapy When the Child is the Referred Patient: II. Methodology and Results. (328)

Brief Therapy with Couples. (113)

Can Families Survive Incest? (405)

Case Report: Smuggling Family Therapy Through. (433)

Case Studies in the Family Treatment of Drug Abuse. (221)

Changes in Self-Concept and Perception of Parental Behavior Among Learning Disabled Elementary School Children as a Result of Parent Effectiveness Training. (315)

Changes in Sibling Behavior Following Family Intervention. (291)

Changing Families: A Family Therapy Reader. (26)

Character-Disordered Family--A Community Treatment Model for Family Sexual Abuse. (67)

Charting as a Multipurpose Treatment Intervention for Family Therapy. (177)

Child Abuse: A Plan for Prevention. (452)

Child Abuse: Where Do We Go From Here? (441)

Child Sexual Abuse: Analysis of a Family Therapy Approach. (190)

Child Therapy Conducted Through Family Therapy. (227)

Child Welfare Agency Project--Therapy for Families of Status Offenders. (338)

Childhood Asthma. A Controlled Trial of Family Psychotherapy. (332)

Children of Alcoholic Parents. (402)

Circumplex Model of Marital and Family System: I. Cohesion and Adaptability Dimensions, Family Types, and Clinical Applications. (47)

Circumplex Model of Marital and Family Systems: III. Empirical Evaluation with Families. (348)

Client-Centered Approaches to Working with the Family: An Overview of New Developments in Therapeutic, Educational, and Preventive Methods. (42)

Collateral Therapy for the Abused Child and the Problem Parent. (89)

Commitment to People: An Evaluation of the Family Reception Center. (424)

Community-Family Network Therapy in a Rural Setting. (108)

A Comparison of Four Behavioral Treatments of Alcoholism. (320)

Conjoint Alcohol Family Therapy Services for Occupational Alcoholism Programs. (419)

Conjoint Marital Therapy: A Controlled Outcome Study. (306)

Conjoint Therapy for Marital Problems. (168)

A Contextual Approach to Treatment of Juvenile Offenders. (173)

Contingency Contracting with Families of Delinquent Adolescents. (366)

The Differential Impact of Work-Oriented Communication-Oriented Juvenile Correction Programs Upon Recidivism Rates in Delinquent Males. (334)

Difficulties in Family Therapy Evaluation. I. A Comparison of Insight vs. Problem-Solving Approaches. II. Design Critique and Recommendations. (351)

Direct Open Supervision: A Team Approach. (418)

Discussion: The Narcissism of Small Differences--and Some Big Ones. (225)

Domestic Violence Assistance Organizations--Summary Report. (342)

Dream Analysis in Family Therapy. (78)

Drug and Family Therapy in the Aftercare of Acute Schizophrenics. (316)

Dynamics of the Pathological Family System. (72)

Dysfunction in the Evangelical Family: Treatment Considerations. (193)

An Eclectic View of Family Therapy: When Is Family Therapy the Treatment of Choice? When Is It Not? (115)

Ecosystemic Epistemology: An Alternative Paradigm for Diagnosis. (37)

The Effectiveness of Family Therapy: A Review of Outcome Research. (307)

Effectiveness Training--A Model for Prevention of Juvenile Crime. (451)

Effects of Alcoholism on the Family System. (257)

Effects of Alcoholism on the Family System. (267)

Effects of Crisis Intervention Counseling on Predelinquent Misdemeanor Juvenile Offenders. (361)

Effects of Short-Term Family Therapy on Patterns of
Verbal Interchange in Disturbed Families. (325)

Elimination of Stealing by Self-Reinforcement of Alternative
Behavior and Family Contracting. (268)

The Emotional and Political Hazards of Teaching and
Learning Family Therapy. (410)

Engagement of the Family in the Treatment of the Hispanic
Alcoholic: Two Miami Programs. (238)

Episodic Dyscontrol and Family Dynamics. (150)

The Establishment of a Therapeutic Alliance with Parents
of Psychiatrically Hospitalized Children. (92)

Evaluating Empathy Skill Training for Parents. (362)

Evaluation of Parent Education Programs. (363)

Experimenting with Family Treatment Approaches to
Alcoholism, 1950-1975: A Review. (357)

An Exploratory Study Evaluating a Behavioral Approach to
Disrupted Family Interactions. (302)

Extended Family Presents. (104)

Fairfax County--Evaluation of the Family Systems Program
Through December 1976. (311)

Families and Family Therapy. (45)

Families and Hospitals: Collusion or Cooperation? (151)

Families in the Treatment of Alcoholism. (323)

The Families of Drug Abusers: A Literature Review. (319)

Family and Marriage Education "Recording." (396)

The Family and the Problem of Internalization. (220)

The Family and the School: Utilizing Human Resources to Promote Learning. (272)

The Family Angel: The Scapegoat's Counterpart. (148)

The Family APGAR: A Proposal for Family Function Test and its Use by Physicians. (259)

A Family Approach to Alcoholism. (85)

The Family as a Social Service: Implications for Policy and Practice. (218)

The Family as a System in Conflict. (58)

The Family as a System in Hospital-Based Social Work. (226)

The Family as a System: Fact or Fantasy. (140)

Family as a Vehicle for Confronting Drug/Alcohol Crisis. (105)

Family Awareness for Nonclinicians: Participation in a Simulated Family as a Teaching Technique. (434)

Family Behavior and Alcoholism. (65)

Family Behavior Modification. (62)

A Family Centered Approach to Residential Care. (205)

Family Counseling and Diversion; Planning and Implementing Programs for Juveniles: Final Report. (275)

Family Counseling as a Key to Successful Alternative School Programs for Alienated Youth. (406)

Family Counseling as an Alternative to Legal Action for the Juvenile Status Offender. (295)

Family Counseling. (49)

Family Counselors and Law Enforcement--Hayward's (CA) Approach to Domestic Violence. (346)

Family Crisis Intervention Program--Clark County, Washington. (379)

Family Education to Enhance the Moral Atmosphere of the Family and the Moral Development of Adolescents. (353)

Family Factbook. (459)

Family Factors in the Etiology and Treatment of Youthful Drug Abuse. (234)

Family Focused Treatment and Management: A Multi-Discipline Training Approach. (131)

Family Illness: Chemical Dependency. (282)

Family in Medical and Psychiatric Treatment: Selected Clinical Approaches. (81)

The Family Interactional Perspective: A Study and Examination of the Work of Don D. Jackson. (19)

Family Intervention for Beginners: A Rationale for a Brief Problem-Oriented Approach in Child and Family Psychiatry. (387)

The Family Life Cycle and Clinical Intervention. (33)

Family Management in the Treatment of Alcoholism. (130)

Family Meal-Time Interaction: Understanding the Family in Its Natural Setting. (194)

Family Members' Perceptions and Use of Time: An Element in Family Treatment. (79)

Family of Origin as a Therapeutic Resource for Adults in Marital and Family Therapy: You Can and Should Go Home Again. (138)

Family Outreach: A Program for the Prevention of Child Neglect and Abuse. (465)

The Family Pride Factor in Family Therapy. (124)

Family Psychotherapy Within Social Psychiatry. (216)

Family Rehabilitation Coordinator Training for In-Home Recovery Assistance Services to Alcoholic Mothers, Their Children and Families. (393)

Family Research Study at Eagleville Hospital and Rehabilitation Center. (373)

Family Resistance to Therapy: A Model for Services and Therapists' Roles. (196)

Family Resource Center: A Family Intervention Approach. (246)

A Family Response to the Drug Problem. (464)

Family Sculpture and Relationship Mapping Techniques. (106)

Family Secrets: The Experience of Emotional Crisis. (240)

Family Sexual Abuse. (378)

The Family Stress Consultation Team: An Illinois Approach to Protective Services. (409)

Family Systems Approach to Child Abuse--Etiology and Intervention. (147)

A Family Systems Approach to Treatment of Child Abuse. (203)

Family Systems Drawings. (285)

Family Systems Perspective in Work with Juvenile Delinquents, Status Offenders, and Dependent Youth: Outcome and Process Evaluation of Training. (369)

Family Theory and Therapy. (15)

Family Theory as a Necessary Component of Family Therapy. (41)

The Family Therapist Behavior Scale (FTBS):
Development and Evaluation of a Coding System. (345)

A Family Therapist Looks· at the Problem of
Incest. (254)

Family Therapy and Drug Abuse: A National
Survey. (303)

Family Therapy and Schizophrenia. (365)

Family Therapy and Sex Role Stereotypes. (152)

Family Therapy and Social Change. (29)

Family Therapy and the Treatment of Drug Abuse
Problems. (163)

A Family Therapy Approach to Alcoholism. (256)

A Family Therapy Approach to the Treatment of Drug
and Alcohol Abuse. (159)

Family Therapy as a Defense. (280)

Family Therapy as a Treatment for Children: A Critical
Review of Outcome Research. (335)

Family Therapy as Reciprocal Emotional Induction. (80)

Family Therapy as Seen by a Group Therapist. (50)

Family Therapy Conceptualization and Use of Case
Notes. (426)

Family Therapy for the Drug User: Conceptual and
Practical Considerations. (110)

Family Therapy for the Trainee in Family Therapy. (399)

Family Therapy in Alcoholism. (265)

Family Therapy in Alcoholism. (31)

Family Therapy in Child and Adolescent Psychiatry: A Review of Families. (336)

Family Therapy in the Black Community. (207)

Family Therapy of Alcoholism. (119)

The Family Therapy of Attempted Suicide. (236)

Family Therapy of Drug and Alcohol Abuse. (327)

Family Therapy Techniques for the Family Physician. (112)

Family Therapy Training in Israel. (436)

Family Therapy with Adolescent Drug Abusers: A Review. (68)

Family Therapy with Black Families: Social Workers' and Clients' Perception. (228)

Family Therapy with Black, Disadvantaged Families: Some Observations on Roles, Communication, and Technique. (134)

Family Therapy with Court-Committed, Institutionalized, Acting-Out Male Adolescents. (386)

Family Therapy with Families Having Delinquent Offspring. (174)

Family Therapy Workshop: When the Family and the Therapist are of Different Races. (157)

Family Therapy. (212)

Family Therapy--A Summary of Selected Literature. (262)

Family Therapy--An Innovative Approach in the Rehabilitation of Adult Probationers. (283)

Family Therapy, Group Therapy. (7)

Family Therapy: A Client-Centered Perspective. (43)

Family Therapy: A Comparison of Approaches. (34)

Family Therapy: A Phenomenological and Active Directive Approach. (11)

Family Therapy: A Summary of Selected Literature. (352)

Family Therapy: Clinical Hodgepodge or Clinical Science. (64)

Family Therapy: Full Length Case Studies. (224)

Family Therapy: Its Role in the Prevention of Criminality. (448)

Family Therapy: The Making of a Mental Health Movement. (9)

Family Therapy: The Single Parent Family and the Battered Child. (286)

Family Therapy: Theory and Practice. (21)

Family Thinking in Prevention of Alcoholism. (466)

Family Treatment Approaches to Drug Abuse Problems: A Review. (354)

Family Treatment for Alcoholism: A Review. (170)

Family Treatment of Drug Problems. (355)

Family Violence: A Psychiatric Perspective. (391)

Family-Centered Group Care. (395)

Family-Focused Management: Treatment of Choice for Deviant and Dependent Families. (129)

A Family-Oriented Psychiatric Inpatient Unit. (401)

Family, Alcohol Misuse, and Alcoholism: Priorities and
Proposals for Intervention.   (127)

The Fear of Committing Child Abuse: A Discussion of
Eight Families.   (287)

A Feminist Approach to Family Therapy.   (153)

Fixation and Regression in the Family Life Cycle.   (4)

Force and Violence in the Family.   (17)

Forced Holding: A Technique for Treating Parentified
Children.   (172)

From Object Relations to Attachment Theory: A Basis for
Family Therapy.   (30)

A Functional Approach to Family Assessment.   (102)

Generation After Generation: The Long-Term Treatment of
an Irish Family with Widespread Alcoholism Over Multiple
Generations.   (101)

Gestalt Approaches to Conjoint Therapy.   (183)

The Greek Chorus and Other Techniques of Paradoxical
Therapy.   (223)

Group Approaches to Treating Marital Problems.   (57)

Group Therapy Intervention Strategies for Abusing Parents and Evaluation of Results.   (176)

Group Therapy with Abusive Parents.   (211)

Group Work with Abuse Parents.   (457)

Guidelines for Family Interviewing and Brief Therapy by
the Family Physician.   (94)

Hazelden: Evaluation of a Residential Family
Program.   (197)

Healthy Family Systems.   (3)

Helping Juveniles by Helping Their Families. (184)

Helping Parents Help Their Children. (440)

Helping People in Crisis. (230)

Helping Youth and Families of Separation, Divorce, and Remarriage: A Program Manual. (432)

Heroin Addiction as a Family Phenomenon: A New Conceptual Model. (60)

High Impact Family Treatment--A Progress Report. (69)

The Home Observation Assessment Metod (HOAM): Real-Time Naturalistic Observation of Families in Their Homes. (266)

Home-Based Services for Children and Families: Policy, Practice, and Research. (460)

Homeostasis and Family Myth: An Overview of the Literature. (260)

Homeostasis. (10)

Homeostasis: A Key Concept in Working with Alcoholic Families. (128)

Homicide and the Family. (298)

Hooking the Involuntary Family into Treatment: Family Therapy in a Juvenile Court Setting. (175)

How Should Families Be Involved in Service Delivery: A Public Agency's Point of View. (392)

Humanistic Treatment of Father-Daughter Incest. (145)

Ideologies, Idols (and Graven Images?): Rejoinder to Gurman and Kniskern. (63)

Impact of Family Systems Intervention on Recidivism and Sibling Delinquency--A Model of Primary Prevention and Program Evaluation. (38)

The Impact of Parent Effectiveness Training on Parent Attitudes and Children's Behavior. (333)

Impact of Stress on the Puerto Rican Family: Treatment Considerations. (100)

An Index for Measuring Agency Involvement in Family Therapy. (305)

Individual and Family Growth: A Gestalt Approach. (36)

Influence of Separate Interviews on Clinicians' Evaluative Perceptions in Family Therapy. (314)

Integrating Services for Troubled Families: Dilemmas of Program Design and Implementation. (435)

The Interaction of Family Therapy and Psychodynamic Individual Therapy in an Inpatient Setting. (91)

An Interactional Approach to Dysfunctional Silencing in Family Therapy. (93)

Intergenerational Separation Anxiety in Family Therapy. (199)

Intergenerational Treatment Approach: An Alternative Model of Working with Abusive/Neglectful and Delinquent Prone Families. (233)

Intervening Briefly in the Family System. (181)

Intra- and Interpersonal Process in the Group Supervision of Family Therapists. (431)

Iowa Research in Family Therapy with Families of Delinquent Youth--Final Report. (337)

Issues in the Implementation of the Parent Aide Concept. (442)

Juvenile Diversion Through Family Counseling--An Exemplary Project. (294)

Juvenile Services Project--An Experiment in Delinquency Control. (300)

Keith: A Case Study of Structural Family Therapy. (156)

Kinetic Psychotherapy in the Treatment of Families. (251)

Kiss the Frog: A Therapeutic Intervention for Reframing Family Rules. (125)

Learning Family Therapy Through Simulation. (382)

Learning for Health Program, Center for Counseling and Psychotherapy, Santa Monica, California. (200)

Learning for Living: A Program Prepared for Use in a Group Home for Children: Leader's Guide. (450)

Learning Multiple Family Therapy Through Simulated Workshops. (420)

Leaving Home: The Therapy of Disturbed Young People. (149)

Limitations of Family Therapy. (247)

The Little Girl, The Family Therapist, and the Fairy-Tale; A True Fable: Based on an Intensive Family Therapy with a Low Socioeconomic Level Family Where a Little Child Was Identified Patient. (245)

The Male Spouse in Marital and Family Therapy. (235)

Mandatory Parental Involvement in the Treatment of Delinquent Youth. (35)

The Many Dimensions of Family Practice: Proceedings of the North American Symposium on Family Practice, November, 1978. (12)

Marital Group Therapy in Alcoholism Treatment. (98)

Marital Therapy of Women Alcoholics. (116)

Marital Violence: Dimensions of the Problem and Modes of Intervention. (249)

Marriage Contracts and Couples Therapy: Hidden Forces in Intimate Relationships. (248)

Meeting Families' Treatment Needs Through a Family Psychotherapy Center. (296)

A Method of Co-Therapy for Schizophrenic Families. (219)

A Model for a Family Systems Theory Approach to Prevention and Treatment of Alcohol Abusing Youth. (56)

Multidisciplinary Approach to the Treatment of Child Abuse. (394)

Multidisciplinary Teams in Child Abuse and Neglect Programs: A Special Report from the National Center on Child Abuse and Neglect. (421)

Multiple Family Group Therapy with a Tri-Therapist Team. (136)

Multiple Family Group Therapy: A Review of the Literature. (61)

Multiple Family Therapy on an Alcohol Treatment Unit. (209)

Multiple Family Therapy Systems. (82)

Multiple Family Therapy: A Literature Review. (14)

Multiple Family Therapy: A New Direction in the Treatment of Drug Abusers. (180)

A Multi-Method Investigation of Two Family Constructs. (330)

Networking Families in Crisis: Intervention Strategies with Families and Social Networks. (51)

New Directions: The Family Center Youth Program, Santa Barbara, California. (415)

Nonverbal Assessment of Family Systems: A Preliminary Study. (120)

Observations of Conjointly Hospitalized "Alcoholic Couples" During Sobriety and Intoxication: Implications for Theory and Therapy. (359)

Occupational Therapy and Child Abuse. (388)

On Shame and the Family. (142)

On the Management of Conflict in Families. (59)

On the Reclaiming of Denied Affects in Family Therapy. (87)

The Optimist-Pessimist Technique. (114)

Organizing Concepts in Family Therapy. (48)

Out of My Practice: The Marriage, Family, and Child Counselor and Public Education. (467)

Overview of the Parents Anonymous Self-Help for Child Abusing Parents Project Evaluation Study for 1974-1976. (470)

Paradox as a Therapeutic Technique: A Review. (55)

The Paradoxes of Intimacy. (191)

Paradoxical Tasks in Family Therapy: Who Can Resist. (154)

Paraprofessionals Providing Behavioral Techniques to Families of Disadvantaged Toddlers. (455)

Parent Awareness Training: Positive Parenting for the 1980's. (458)

Parent Education and Intervention Handbook. (437)

Parent Education and Parent Involvement: Retrospect and Prospect. (449)

Parent Group Education and Student Self-Esteem. (349)

Parent Group Training Programs in Juvenile Courts: A National Survey. (368)

Parenting in a Multicultural Society. (447)

Parenting Skills Workbook. (439)

Parenting Skills: Trainer's Manual. (438)

Parents Anonymous: A Treatment Method for Child Abuse. (453)

Parents as Treatment Partners in Residential Care. (189)

Patterns of Redundancy in Marriage and Family Systems. (70)

Peer Group Supervision in Family Therapy. (376)

Pilgrim's Progress III: A Trend Analysis of Family Theory and Methodology. (32)

A Plan for Identifying Priorities in Treating Multiproblem Families. (97)

The Practice of Conjoint Therapy. (107)

Pre-marriage Contracts: An Aid to Couples Living with Parents. (239)

Predictions of Therapeutic Process in Conjoint Family Therapy. (347)

Prevention and/or Treatment of Child Abuse and Neglect in Head Start--an Eclectic, Ecologic Hypothesis. (461)

Probation Officers, Family Crisis Counseling, and Juvenile Diversion, Parts 1 and 2. (73)

Problem-Solving Therapy: New Strategies for Effective Family Therapy. (27)

Research into Family Factors in Alcoholism. (289)

Research: Alcohol as a Member of the Family. (358)

Residential Family Therapy. (375)

The Resonating Parental Bind and Delinquency. (160)

Resources for Help in Parenting. (469)

Results of Family Therapy with Juvenile Offenders. (326)

The Results of Family Therapy Revisited: The Nonbehavioral Methods. (367)

A Review of the Literature Related to Family Therapy in the Black Community. (208)

A Ritualized Prescription in Family Therapy: Odd Days and Even Days. (222)

The Role of Goal Attainment Scaling in Evaluating Family Therapy Outcome. (371)

The Search for Reinforcers to Training and Maintaining Effective Parent Behaviors. (75)

Searching for the Magic Answer to Juvenile Delinquency. (428)

Selection Criteria for Family Therapy. (103)

Severe Female Delinquency--When to Involve the Family in Treatment. (96)

Sharing the Crisis of Rape: Counseling the Mates and Families of Victims. (258)

A Short Term Community Based Early Stage Intervention Program for Behavior Problem Youth. (299)

Sib Group Therapy: A Prevention Program for Siblings from Drug-Addicted Families. (444)

Sibling Therapy. (231)

Similarities in Families of Drug Dependents and
Alcoholics. (374)

The Simulated Family as an Aid to Learning Family Group
Treatment. (384)

Sisterhood-Brotherhood is Powerful: Sibling Sub-Systems
and Family Therapy. (71)

Social Dimension of Family Treatment. (46)

Solitary Toy Play and Time Out: A Family Treatment
Package for Children with Aggressive and Oppositional
Behavior. (364)

Some Notes on the Use of Family Sculpture in
Therapy. (171)

St. Croix: An Outpatient Family Treatment
Approach. (99)

Stepfamilies: A Guide to Working with Stepparents and
Stepchildren. (278)

A Stepfamily in Formation. (232)

Strategies of Family Therapy in Probation Assistance--
Necessity and Concept. (252)

Structural Family Therapy: One Approach to the
Treatment of the Alcoholic Family. (135)

A Study of Conceptualization of Family Structure by
Experienced Family Therapists. (356)

A Study of the Relationship Between Family Interaction and
Individual Symptomology Over Time. (360)

Substance Abuse and Family Interaction. (185)

Successful Short-Term Family Therapy with Incarcerated
Adolescents. (297)

Susan Smiled: On Examplation in Family Therapy. (52)

Symbiosis, Empathy, Suicidal Behavior, and the Family. (237)

Systematic Parent Training: Procedures, Cases, and Issues. (215)

A Systems Approach to Family Therapy. (16)

Systems of Family and Marital Psychotherapy. (54)

Systems Specifics in "Break-In"--A Therapeutic Approach. (18)

Systems-Behavioral Intervention with Families of Delinquents--Therapist Characteristics: Family Behavior and Outcome. (66)

Tavistock Family Therapy Conference: A Review. (187)

Teaching Family Psychodynamics in a Family Practice Center: One Experience. (400)

Teaching Family Therapy by Simulation. (425)

Teaching Family Therapy to Social Work Students. (423)

The Teaching of Family Therapy Skills on an In-Patient Child Psychiatry Ward. (422)

Team Treatment for Abusive Families. (381)

A Technique for Reducing Parental Obsessions in Family Therapy. (143)

Techniques of Brief Therapy with Children and Parents. (121)

Technolatry, Methodolatry, and the Results of Family Therapy. (23)

Tender Loving Care: A Program Prepared for Mother-Baby and Maternity Centers of the Salvation Army: Leader's Guide. (468)

Theory and Practice in Matching Treating to the Special Characteristics and Problems of Cuban Immigrants. (270)

Therapeutic Mobilization of Families Around Drug-Induced Adolescent Crises. (261)

Therapeutic Strategies in Conjoint Hospitalization for the Treatment of Alcoholism. (111)

Therapeutic Systems and Settings in the Treatment of Child Abuse. (83)

Therapeutic Videotaped Playback: A Critical Review. (322)

Therapist, Save My Child: A Family Crisis Case. (90)

Therapists' Perceptions of Healthy Family Functioning. (313)

Therapists' Relationship with Couples with an Alcoholic Member. (86)

Therapists' Skills as Determinants of Effective Systems-Behavioral Family Therapy. (74)

Three Assessment Tools for Family Therapy. (217)

Three Models of Family Therapy: Prevention, Crisis Treatment, or Rehabilitation. (40)

Through the Looking Glass: The Experiences of Two Family Therapy Trainees with Live Supervision. (398)

A Time-Limited Treatment Program for Children and Their Families. (416)

Toward a Metacommunicational Framework of Couple Interactions. (88)

Toward Systemic Diagnosis. (182)

Trainee Response to Family Therapy Training. (427)

Training Abusive Parents in Child Management and Self-Control Skills. (446)

Training Community-Based Paraprofessionals as Behavior Therapists with Families of Alcohol-Abusing Adolescents. (429)

Training Family Psychologists: The Family Studies Program at Georgia State University. (408)

Training in Family Therapy: Perceptual, Conceptual, and Executive Skills. (430)

Training in Family Treatment: Needs and Objectives. (377)

Training Parents as Mental Health Agents. (445)

Training Undergraduates as Co-Leaders of Multifamily Counseling Groups. (407)

Transfer of Therapeutic Effects from Institution to Home: Faith, Hope, and Behavior Modification. (161)

Treating Chronic Crisis Bearers and Their Families. (118)

Treating Dysfunctional Families at Home. (385)

Treating the Adolescent Drug Abuser: A Family Affair. (167)

Treating the Family. (229)

Treating the Parents of Adolescent Drug Abusers. (165)

Treating the Parents of Adolescent Drug Abusers. (166)

A Treatment Approach to Child Abuse and Delinquency. (279)

The Treatment of Sexual Problems in Marital and Family Therapy. (213)

Treatment of the Significant Other. (162)

Treatment Program for Abused Children and Their Families in Conjunction with Nursing Education. (403)

Triads and the Drug-Dependent Mother. (139)

Two Is Better Than One: Use of Behavioral Techniques Within a Structural Family Therapy Model. (243)

A Typology of Family Social Environments. (339)

Uncommon Therapy: The Psychiatric Techniques of Milton H. Erickson, M.D. (28)

Understanding the Role of Extrafamilial Social Forces in Family Treatment: A Critique of Family Therapy. (39)

The Upward Mobile Negro Family in Therapy. (210)

The Use of Family Therapy in Drug Abuse Treatment: A National Survey. (341)

The Use of Live Consultation in Family Therapy. (95)

The Use of Teaching Stories in Conjoint Family Therapy. (13)

Use of the Extended Family in the Treatment of Multiple Personality. (77)

The Use of the Mini-Contract in Family Therapy. (146)

The Use of the One-Way Mirror in Restructuring Family Boundaries. (144)

The Use of Time in Family Therapy. (141)

The User of Self as a Family Therapist. (186)

What To Say When. (202)

Working From the Outside: Administrative Considerations in the Psychotherapy of a Family with Disrupted Boundaries. (164)

Working with Families of Children in Residential
Treatment. (411)

Working with Parents of Abused and Neglected Children:
A Counseling Approach for Professionals and Lay
People. (206)

Youth Diversion and the Myth of Parental
Indifference. (255)

Youth Service Center--Second Chance for the Youthful
Offender. (310)

the story of the family told in ancient symbols

man

the woman becomes pregnant,

woman

and bears a child.

man and woman united for procreation.

the family; man with
his wife and children.

the man dies.

the forlorn mother with her remaining child.

the widow and her children.

the mother dies,

one child dies.

leaving one surviving child, bearing
within himself the germ of a new family.